FTCE Math

Practice Test Questions for FTCE Mathematics 6 - 12 Test

Published by

Complete TEST
Preparation Inc.

Published by
Complete Test Preparation Inc.
Victoria BC Canada

Visit us on the web at http://www.test-preparation.ca
Printed in the USA

ISBN-13: 9781772451696

Version 6.6 February 2017

About Complete Test Preparation

The Complete Test Preparation Team has been publishing high quality study materials since 2005. Thousands of students visit our websites every year, and thousands of students, teachers and parents all over the world have purchased our teaching materials, curriculum, study guides and practice tests.

Complete Test Preparation is committed to providing students with the best study materials and practice tests available on the market. Members of our team combine years of teaching experience, with experienced writers and editors, all with advanced degrees.

Feedback

We welcome your feedback. Email us at feedback@test-preparation.ca with your comments and suggestions. We carefully review all suggestions and often incorporate reader suggestions into upcoming versions. As a Print on Demand Publisher, we update our products frequently.

Find us on Facebook

www.facebook.com/CompleteTestPreparation

The Environment and Sustainability

Environmental consciousness is important for the continued growth of our company. In addition to eco-balancing each title, as a print on demand publisher, we only print units as orders come in, which greatly reduces excess printing and waste. This revolutionary printing technology also eliminates carbon emissions from trucks hauling boxes of books everywhere to warehouses. We also maintain a commitment to recycling any waste materials that may result from the printing process. We continue to review our manufacturing practices on an ongoing basis to ensure we are doing our part to protect and improve the environment.

Contents

6   **Getting Started**
The FTCE Math 6 - 9 Study Plan   8
Making a Study Schedule   8

13   **Practice Test Questions Set 1**
Answer Key   54

97   **Practice Test Questions Set 2**
Answer Key   137

180   **Conclusion**

Getting Started

CONGRATULATIONS! By deciding to take the FTCE Mathematics Test, you have taken the first step toward a great future! Of course, there is no point in taking this important examination unless you intend to do your very best to earn the highest grade you possibly can. That means getting yourself organized and discovering the best approaches, methods and strategies to master the material. Yes, that will require real effort and dedication on your part, however, if you are willing to focus your energy and devote the study time necessary, before you know it you will be on you will be passing your exam with a great mark!

We know that taking on a new endeavour can be a little scary, and it is easy to feel unsure of where to begin. That's where we come in.

About the Exam

The FTCE Mathematics Test is composed of eight content areas, Algebra, (Basic and Advanced), Functions, Geometry, Trigonometry, Statistics and Probability, Calculus and Mathematical Reasoning.

While we seek to make our guide as comprehensive as possible, note that like all exams, the FTCE Mathematics Test might be adjusted at some future point. New material might be added, or content that is no longer relevant or applicable might be removed. It is always a good idea to give the materials you receive when you register to take the FTCE Mathematics a careful review.

The FTCE Mathematics Study Plan

Now that you have made the decision to take the FTCE Mathematics, it is time to get started. Before you do another thing, you will need to figure out a plan of attack. The very best study tip is to start early! The longer the time period you devote to regular study practice, the more likely you will be to retain the material and be able to access it quickly. If you thought that 1x20 is the same as 2x10, guess what? It really is not, when it comes to study time. Reviewing material for just an hour per day over the course of 20 days is far better than studying for two hours a day for only 10 days. The more often you revisit a particular piece of information, the better you will know it. Not only will your grasp and understanding be better, but your ability to reach into your brain and quickly and efficiently pull out the tidbit you need, will be greatly enhanced as well.

The great Chinese scholar and philosopher Confucius believed that true knowledge could be defined as knowing both what you know and what you do not know. The first step in preparing for the FTCE Mathematics is to assess your strengths and weaknesses.

Making a Study Schedule

To make your study time the most productive you will need to develop a study plan. The purpose of the plan is to organize all the bits of pieces of information in such a way that you will not feel overwhelmed. Rome was not built in a day, and learning everything you will need to know to pass the FTCE Mathematics is going to take time, too. Arranging the material you need to learn into manageable chunks is the best way to go. Each study session should make you feel as though you have succeeded in accomplishing your goal, and your goal is simply to learn what you planned to learn during that particular session. Try to organize the content in such a way that each study session builds on previous ones. That way, you will retain the information, be better able to access it, and review the previous bits and pieces at the same time.

Self-assessment

The Best Study Tip! The very best study tip is to start early! The longer you study regularly, the more you will retain and 'learn' the material. Studying for 1 hour per day for 20 days is far better than studying for 2 hours for 10 days.

What don't you know?

The first step is to assess your strengths and weaknesses. You may already have an idea of where your weaknesses are, or you can take our Self-assessment modules for each of the areas, Reading Comprehension, Arithmetic, Essay Writing, Algebra and College Level Math.

Exam Component	Rate 1 to 5
Trigonometry	
Algebra	
Functions	
Calculus	
Geometry	
Statistics and Probability	
Mathematical Reasoning	

Making a Study Schedule

The key to making a study plan is to divide the material you need to learn into manageable size and learn it, while at the same time reviewing the material that you already know.

Using the table above, any scores of three or below, you need to spend time learning, going over and practicing this subject area. A score of four means you need to review the material, but you don't have to spend time re-learning. A score of five and you are OK with just an occasional review before the exam.

A score of zero or one means you really do need to work on this and you should allocate the most time and give it the highest priority. Some students prefer a 5-day plan and others a 10-day plan. It also depends on how much time you have until the exam.

Here is an example of a 5-day plan based on an example from the table above:

Trigonometry: 1   Study 1 hour everyday – review on last day

Algebra: 3   Study 1 hour for 2 days then ½ hour and then review

Functions: 4   Review every second day

Geometry: 2 Study 1 hour on the first day – then ½ hour everyday

Statistics and Probability: 5   Review for ½ hour every other day

Using this example, Geometry and Statistics and Probability are good and only need occasional review. Functions are good and needs 'some' review. Algebra needs a bit of work and Trigonometry is very weak and needs the most time. Based on this, here is a sample study plan:

Day	Subject	Time
Monday		
Study	Trigonometry	1 hour
Study	Geometry	1 hour
	½ hour break	
Study	Algebra	1 hour
Review	Functions	½ hour
Tuesday		
Study	Trigonometry	1 hour
Study	Geometry	½ hour
	½ hour break	
Study	Algebra	½ hour
Review	Functions	½ hour
Wednes-day		
Study	Trigonometry	1 hour
Study	Geometry	½ hour
	½ hour break	
Study	Algebra	½ hour
Thursday		
Study	Trigonometry	½ hour
Study	Geometry	½ hour
Review	Algebra	½ hour
	½ hour break	
Review	Functions	½ hour
Friday		
Review	Trigonometry	½ hour
Review	Geometry	½ hour
Review	Algebra	½ hour
	½ hour break	
Review	Functions	½ hour
Review	Geometry	½ hour

Using this example, adapt the study plan to your own schedule. This schedule assumes 2 ½ - 3 hours available to study everyday for a 5 day period.

First, write out what you need to study and how much. Next figure out how many days you have before the test. Note, do NOT study on the last day before the test. On the last day before the test, you won't learn anything and will probably only confuse yourself.

Make a table with the days before the test and the number of hours you have available to study each day. We suggest working with 1 hour and ½ hour time slots.

Start filling in the blanks, with the subjects you need to study the most getting the most time and the most regular time slots (i.e. everyday) and the subjects that you know getting the least time (e.g. ½ hour every other day, or every 3rd day).

Tips for making a schedule

Once you make a schedule, stick with it! Make your study sessions reasonable. If you make a study schedule and don't stick with it, you set yourself up for failure. Instead, schedule study sessions that are a bit shorter and set yourself up for success! Make sure your study sessions are do-able. Studying is hard work but after you pass, you can party and take a break!

Schedule breaks. Breaks are just as important as study time. Work out a rotation of studying and breaks that works for you.

Build up study time. If you find it hard to sit still and study for 1 hour straight-through, build up to it. Start with 20 minutes, and then take a break. Once you get used to 20-minute study sessions, increase the time to 30 minutes. Gradually work you way up to 1 hour.

40 minutes to 1 hour is optimal. Studying for longer than this is tiring and not productive. Studying for shorter isn't long enough to be productive.

Practice Test Questions Set 1

The questions below are not the same as you will find on the FTCE Mathematics - that would be too easy! And nobody knows what the questions will be and they change all the time. Below are general questions that cover the same subject areas as the FTCE Mathematics test. So, while the format and exact wording of the questions may differ slightly, and change from year to year, if you can answer the questions below, you will have no problem with the FTCE Mathematics test.

For the best results, take these practice test questions as if it were the real exam. Set aside time when you will not be disturbed, and a location that is quiet and free of distractions. Read the instructions carefully, read each question carefully, and answer to the best of your ability.
Use the bubble answer sheets provided. When you have completed the practice questions, check your answer against the Answer Key and read the explanation provided.

Do not attempt more than one set of practice test questions in one day. After completing the first practice test, wait two or three days before attempting the second set of questions.

Algebra Answer Sheet

1. (A) (B) (C) (D)   11. (A) (B) (C) (D)

2. (A) (B) (C) (D)   12. (A) (B) (C) (D)

3. (A) (B) (C) (D)   13. (A) (B) (C) (D)

4. (A) (B) (C) (D)   14. (A) (B) (C) (D)

5. (A) (B) (C) (D)   15. (A) (B) (C) (D)

6. (A) (B) (C) (D)   16. (A) (B) (C) (D)

7. (A) (B) (C) (D)   17. (A) (B) (C) (D)

8. (A) (B) (C) (D)   18. (A) (B) (C) (D)

9. (A) (B) (C) (D)   19. (A) (B) (C) (D)

10. (A) (B) (C) (D)   20. (A) (B) (C) (D)

Functions Answer Sheet

1. Ⓐ Ⓑ Ⓒ Ⓓ   11. Ⓐ Ⓑ Ⓒ Ⓓ

2. Ⓐ Ⓑ Ⓒ Ⓓ   12. Ⓐ Ⓑ Ⓒ Ⓓ

3. Ⓐ Ⓑ Ⓒ Ⓓ   13. Ⓐ Ⓑ Ⓒ Ⓓ

4. Ⓐ Ⓑ Ⓒ Ⓓ   14. Ⓐ Ⓑ Ⓒ Ⓓ

5. Ⓐ Ⓑ Ⓒ Ⓓ   15. Ⓐ Ⓑ Ⓒ Ⓓ

6. Ⓐ Ⓑ Ⓒ Ⓓ

7. Ⓐ Ⓑ Ⓒ Ⓓ

8. Ⓐ Ⓑ Ⓒ Ⓓ

9. Ⓐ Ⓑ Ⓒ Ⓓ

10. Ⓐ Ⓑ Ⓒ Ⓓ

Geometry Answer Sheet

1. (A) (B) (C) (D)   11. (A) (B) (C) (D)

2. (A) (B) (C) (D)   12. (A) (B) (C) (D)

3. (A) (B) (C) (D)   13. (A) (B) (C) (D)

4. (A) (B) (C) (D)   14. (A) (B) (C) (D)

5. (A) (B) (C) (D)   15. (A) (B) (C) (D)

6. (A) (B) (C) (D)

7. (A) (B) (C) (D)

8. (A) (B) (C) (D)

9. (A) (B) (C) (D)

10. (A) (B) (C) (D)

Trigonometry and Calculus Answer Sheet

1. Ⓐ Ⓑ Ⓒ Ⓓ

2. Ⓐ Ⓑ Ⓒ Ⓓ

3. Ⓐ Ⓑ Ⓒ Ⓓ

4. Ⓐ Ⓑ Ⓒ Ⓓ

5. Ⓐ Ⓑ Ⓒ Ⓓ

6. Ⓐ Ⓑ Ⓒ Ⓓ

7. Ⓐ Ⓑ Ⓒ Ⓓ

8. Ⓐ Ⓑ Ⓒ Ⓓ

9. Ⓐ Ⓑ Ⓒ Ⓓ

10. Ⓐ Ⓑ Ⓒ Ⓓ

Statistics Probability and Mathematical Reasoning Answer Sheet

1. (A) (B) (C) (D)   11. (A) (B) (C) (D)

2. (A) (B) (C) (D)   12. (A) (B) (C) (D)

3. (A) (B) (C) (D)   13. (A) (B) (C) (D)

4. (A) (B) (C) (D)   14. (A) (B) (C) (D)

5. (A) (B) (C) (D)

6. (A) (B) (C) (D)

7. (A) (B) (C) (D)

8. (A) (B) (C) (D)

9. (A) (B) (C) (D)

10. (A) (B) (C) (D)

Part I - Algebra

1. $\sqrt{75} + \sqrt{48} - \sqrt{(3 / 0.01)} =$

    a. $- \sqrt{3}$

    b. $\sqrt{3}$

    c. 3

    d. $3\sqrt{3}$

2. $x = a + bi$ and $y = a - bi$. If $x * y = 5a^2$, find one possible value of b in terms of a.

    a. a

    b. 2a

    c. 3a

    d. 4a

3. Find the determinant of matrix $A = \begin{bmatrix} 2 & -1 & 0 \\ 5 & 3 & 1 \\ 1 & 1 & -2 \end{bmatrix}$

    a. -30

    b. -25

    c. 10

    d. 15

4. Factor the polynomial $x^3y^3 - x^2y^8$.

    a. $x^2y^3(x - y^5)$

    b. $x^3y^3(1 - y^5)$

    c. $x^2y^2(x - y^6)$

    d. $xy^3(x - y^5)$

5. We are given that A = (√3 - 1) / (√5 + 1) and B = (√5 - 1) / (√3 + 1). What is the value of A in terms of B?

    a. B/2

    b. 3B/2

    c. 2B

    d. 3B

6. Using the factoring method, solve the quadratic equation: $x^2 - 5x - 6 = 0$

    a. -6 and 1

    b. -1 and 6

    c. 1 and 6

    d. -6 and -1

7. Find the area of the shape that is between $y \leq 2x + 6$, x-axis and y-axis.

    a. 9 units²

    b. 12 units²

    c. 15 units²

    d. 18 units²

8. Find 2 numbers that sum to 21 and the sum of the squares is 261.

    a. 14 and 7

    b. 15 and 6

    c. 16 and 5

    d. 17 and 4

9. Using the factoring method, solve the quadratic equation: $x^2 + 4x + 4 = 0$

    a. 0 and 1

    b. 1 and 2

    c. 2

    d. -2

10. $(3y^5 - 2y + y^4 + 2y^3 + 5) + (2y^5 + 3y^3 + 2 + 7y)$

    a. $5y^5 + y^4 + 5y^3 + 5y + 7$

    b. $5y^3 + y^4 + 5y^3$

    c. $5y^5 + y^3 + 7y^3 + 5y + 5$

    d. $5y^2 + y^4 + 5y^3 + 7y + 5$

11. $(x^2 - 2)(3x^2 - 3x + 7) =$

    a. $3x^3 - 3x^3 + x^2 + 4x - 12$

    b. $3x^4 - 3x^3 + x^2 + 6x - 14$

    c. $3x^2 - 3x^3 + x + 6x - 10$

    d. $3x^2 - 3x + x + 4x - 14$

12. Find the x-intercepts of the quadratic function $f(x) = (x - 5)^2 - 9$.

    a. {2,4}

    b. {2,8}

    c. {4,8}

    d. {1,2}

13. **Line d_1 is parallel to line d_2, and the equation of line d_2 is y = 3x + 2. Which of the following cannot be the equation of line d_1?**

    a. 3y = 9x - 8

    b. y = -2x + 2

    c. y = 3x + 5

    d. -4y = 5 - 12x

14. **Solve the system: 4x - y = 5; x + 2y = 8**

    a. (3, 2)

    b. (3, 3)

    c. (2, 3)

    d. (2, 2)

15. **Find 2 numbers whose difference is 11 and product is -24. (There is more than one solution.)**

    a. (3,-8)

    b. (-3,8)

    c. (-3,-8)

    d. (3,8)

16. **Find the sides of a right triangle whose sides are consecutive numbers.**

    a. 1, 2, 3

    b. 2, 3, 4

    c. 3, 4, 5

    d. 4, 5, 6

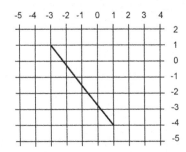

17. What is the slope of the line shown above?

   a. 5/4
   b. -4/5
   c. -5/4
   d. -4/5

18. Driver B drove his car 20 km/h faster than the driver A, and the driver B travelled 480 km 2 hours before driver A. What was the speed of the driver A?

   a. 70
   b. 80
   c. 60
   d. 90

19. The volume of a pool is 7V liters. A tap pours y/4 liters of water per minute. Which of the following is the correct expression showing the time in minutes needed to fill 1/5 of the pool?

   a. 7V/20y
   b. 28V/5y
   c. 28y/5V
   d. 35y/4V

20. If x = $\sqrt{7}$ - 1 and y = $\sqrt{7}$ + 1, find the value of (x + y) / (x - y).

   a. $-\sqrt{7}$

   b. -2

   c. 2

   d. $\sqrt{7}$

Part II - Functions

1. Describe the end behavior for the function f(x) = - 2x^5 + 3x + 97.

   a. Up on the left and right.

   b. Down on the left and right.

   c. Down on the left, up on the right.

   d. Up on the left, down on the right.

2. Given g(x) = x^2 - 2 and h(x) = (x^2 - 2)^3, find the first derivative of the function f(x) = g(x) * h(x).

   a. $4(x^2 - 2)^3$

   b. $8x(x^2 - 2)^3$

   c. $4x^2 - 8$

   d. $(x^2 - 2)^3$

3. Find the antiderivative of 1/x + x^3 - cosx.

   a. $\ln x + x^4/4 + \sin x + C$

   b. $\ln x + x^4 - \sin x + C$

   c. $\ln x + x^4/4 - \sin x + C$

   d. $x^2 + x^4/4 - \sin x + C$

4. The general term of the sequence $\{a_n\}$ is 7^{2n-5}. How many times a_n is equal to a_{n+2}?

 a. 7^{-1}

 b. 7

 c. 7^2

 d. 7^4

5. A function is defined as $f(x) = \begin{cases} x > 1; \ x^3 + 2 \\ x \le 1; \ -x/2 \end{cases}$

What is $(f(1) * f(3) - f(0)) / f^2(2)$ equal to?

 a. 0.130

 b. -0.145

 c. 0.200

 d. -0.240

6. If $f(x) = -x$, $g(x) = 2x + 1$ and $h(x) = x^2$, find $f{\circ}g{\circ}h$.

 a. $x^2 - 1$

 b. $-2x^2 - 1$

 c. $x^2 - 2$

 d. $x^2 + 1$

7. Find the inverse function of the function $f(x) = 3x + 3$.

 a. $(3x - 1)/3$

 b. $(x + 1)/3$

 c. $(x - 1)/3$

 d. $(x - 3)/3$

8. Find the inverse function of the function f(x) = (5x - 2)/4.

    a. (4x - 1)/5

    b. (x + 4)/5

    c. (4x + 2)/5

    d. (4x - 2)/5

9. Find $f^{-1}(1/2)$ if f(x) = 1 - x.

    a. 1

    b. 1/2

    c. 1/3

    d. 1/4

10. Determine the domain and the range of the table below:

x	y
-5	18
4	15
2	9
7	4
12	-3

    a. domain: {- 3, 4, 9, 15, 18} range: {- 5, 4, 2, 7, 12}

    b. domain: {9, 11, 11, 13, 19} range: {- 3, 4, 9, 15, 18}

    c. domain: {- 5, 2, 4, 7, 12} range: {- 3, 4, 9, 15, 18}

    d. domain: {9, 11, 13, 19} range: {- 3, 4, 9, 15, 18}

Part III - Geometry

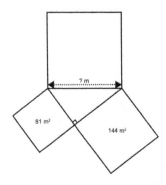

Note: figure not drawn to scale

1. What is the length of each side of the indicated square above? Assume the 3 shapes around the center triangle are square.

    a. 10
    b. 15
    c. 20
    d. 5

2. For triangles ABC and A'B'C' we are given:

BC = B'C'
AC = A'C'

$\angle$ **A** = $\angle$ **A'**

Are these 2 triangles congruent?

    a. Yes

    b. No

    c. Not enough information

3. Reflect the circle with the center in O with the given mirror line m.

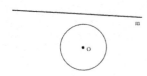

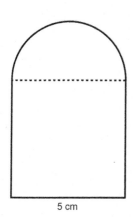

5 cm

Note: figure not drawn to scale

4. What is the perimeter of the above shape, assuming the bottom section is a 5cm square?

    a. 22.85 cm

    b. 20 ⊓ cm

    c. 15 ⊓ cm

d. 25 π cm

5. What is the distance between the two points?

   a. ≈19
   b. 20
   c. ≈21
   d. ≈22

6. If the line m is parallel to the side AB of △ABC, what is angle a?

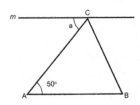

   a. 130°
   b. 25°
   c. 65°
   d. 50°

7. For triangles ABC and A'B'C' we have that:

AB = A'B'

∠ A = ∠ A'
∠ B = ∠ B'

Are these 2 triangles congruent?

    a. Yes
    b. No
    c. Not enough information

8. N is a point inside the circle and [BD] and [AC] are two secants passing through N. If |BN| = 4, |NC| = 14 and |AN| = 2, what is the value of |ND|?

    a. 4
    b. 5
    c. 6
    d. 7

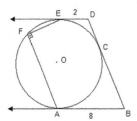

9. In the figure above, [EF] ⊥ [FA], |ED| = 2 cm, |AB| = 8 cm, O is the center of the circle and the circle is tangent to the lines around at points A, C and E. Find the radius of the circle.

    a. 1 cm
    b. 2 cm
    c. 3 cm
    d. 4 cm

10. Find the volume of a cone with radius 5 cm and height 12 cm in m³.

    a. $\pi * 10^{-6}$ m³

    b. $5\pi * 10^{-5}$ m³

    c. $\pi * 10^{-4}$ m³

    d. $12\pi * 10^{-3}$ m³

11. Find the directrix of the graph
y - 5/2 = (-1/2)(x - 2)².

    a. -2

    b. -1

    c. 2

    d. 3

12. Determine the coordinates of the center of the circle given by the equation x² + y² - 6x + 4y + 4 = 0.

    a. (-3, -2)

    b. (3, -2)

    c. (3, 2)

    d. (3, 3)

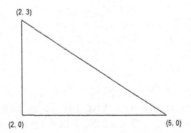

(2, 3)

(2, 0)   (5, 0)

13. If we reflect the triangle with corners on (2, 0), (5, 0), (2, 3) across the x-axis, what will the area of the compound shape be?

    a. 9 units²

    b. 12 units²

    d. 15 units²

    d. 18 units²

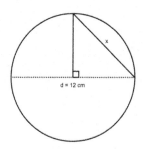

d = 12 cm

Note: Figure not drawn to scale

14. Calculate the length of side x.

    a. 6.46

    b. 8.48

    c. 3.6

    d. 6.4

15. Reflect the parallelogram ABCD with the given mirror line m.

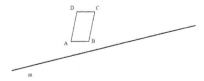

Part IV - Trigonometry

1. What is arccos(1/5) + arcsin(1/5) equal to?

    a. $\pi/4$

    b. $\pi/2$

    c. $3\pi/4$

    d. 2π

2. Find the solution for
(tanx * sinx - cotx * cosx) / (cosx + cscx).

    a. cotx - 1

    b. tanx -1

    c. tanx + 1

    d. 1 + cotx

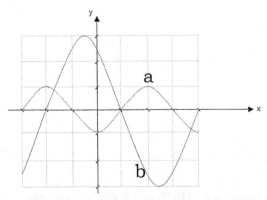

3. Using the period of graph a, and the period of graph b in the figure above, find |b - a|. Assume that the gridlines form equal unit squares.

    a. 1 unit

    b. 2 units

    c. 3 units

    d. 4 units

4. A man builds a triangular pool in the garden. One of the inner angles of the pool is 60⁰ and the side opposite it is 5 m long. Another inner angle is 40⁰. Find the absolute value of the difference between the other two sides of the pool. Round your answer to the nearest thousandths.

    a. 1.805 m

    b. 1.975 m

    c. 2.655 m

    d. 4.325 m

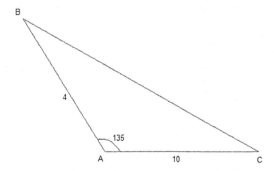

5. Using trigonometric functions, find the area of the triangle above.

    a. 10

    b. 5√2

    c. 20

    d. 20.12

Part VI - Calculus

6. Given that $\int_{-1}^{3} f(x)dx = -15$ and $\int_{3}^{-1} g(x)dx = 8$, find the value of $\int_{-1}^{3}(4g(x) - 5f(x))dx.$

    a. -107

    b. -43

    c. 43

    d. 107

7. Find the following limit: $\lim_{x \to 5} (\tan(x^2 - 25)/(x - 5))$

    a. 2

    b. 5

    c. 10

    d. 25

8. Find the slope of the line tangent to the curve $y = 4\sqrt{x}$ at $x = 2$.

    a. $-\sqrt{2}$

    b. -1

    c. 1

    d. $\sqrt{2}$

9. Given f(x) = (x + 4)², find the interval where the function is increasing.

    a. [-4, 4]
    b. (-∞, -4)
    c. (-4, +∞)
    d. (4, +∞)

10. Find the inflection points of the given function:

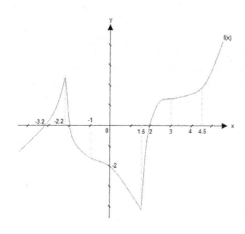

    a. -2.2, 1.5
    b. -1, 3
    c. -3.2, 2
    d. -2

Part V - Statistics and Probability

1. There are 3 blue, 1 white and 4 red identical balls inside a bag. If two balls are taken out of the bag consecutively, what is the probability to have 1 blue and 1 white ball?

> a. 3/28
> b. 1/12
> c. 1/7
> d. 3/7

2. There are 5 blue, 5 green and 5 red books on a shelf. Two books are selected randomly. What is the probability to choose two books of different colors?

> a. 1/3
> b. 2/5
> c. 4/7
> d. 5/7

3. Below is the graph of a exam scores. What is the frequency density of the students getting 62 points? Round your answer to the nearest thousandths.

> a. 0.100
> b. 0.114
> c. 0.200
> d. 0.225

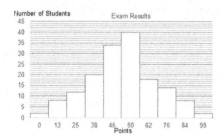

4. In 2014, a survey is conducted to analyze the number of children residents of cities A and B have. Below is the relative frequencies show the results of the study. Total population of city A is approximately 2 million, and city B is 4 million.

	City A	City B
Less than 2 children	0.68	0.57
Equal and more than 2, less than 4 children	0.29	0.42
Equal to and heigher than 4 children	0.03	0.01
Column total	1.00	1.00

According to the study, approximately how many total residents in cities A and B have either no, or 1 child?

    a. 1.2 million

    b. 1.36 million

    c. 2.28 million

    d. 3.64 million

5. A teacher takes a survey only to the students sitting on the front row in his class. What type of bias is observed here?

    a. Self selection bias

    b. Undercoverage bias

    c. Survivorship bias

    d. Voluntary response bias

6. Below is the table of Philip's scores at school and hours of courses per week. Calculate his weighted score.

Course	Credits	Score
A	2	3
B	3	2.5
C	4	4
D	1	1.5
E	1	2.5
F	4	3.5
G	5	3

    a. 2.85

    b. 3

    c. 3.125

    d. 3.2

7. There are 3 chemistry, 2 physics and 5 mathematics books on a shelf. Without separating books of the same category, in how many different ways can we order them in a row?

    a. 3!

    b. $2! * 3! * 5!$

    c. $2! * 3! * 3! * 5!$

    d. $2^{2.3.5}$

Part VII - Mathematical Reasoning

8. What is the contrapositive of the conditional statement "If 3 times a equals 12, then a is an integer?"

a. If a is not an integer, then 3 times a does not equal 12.

b. If a is an integer, then 3 times a equals 12.

c. If 3 times a does not equal 12, then a is not an integer.

d. If a is not an integer, then 3 times a equals 12.

9. Which conditional statement below has a converse with the same truth value?

a. For all integers n; if n is odd, then n^2 is odd.

b. For all real numbers a; if a < 0, then a < 5.

c. If it is a cat, then it has whiskers.

d. If a number is divisible by 5, then it is divisible by 25.

10. Which one of the following statements contain inductive reasoning?

a. My dog barks. The dogs I see in our neighborhood bark. Therefore, every dog barks.

b. Quadrilaterals have four sides. A square has four sides.

c. All apples on the tree are red. With my eyes closed; the apple I pick from the tree is red.

d. The square of a number is found by multiplying the number by itself. The square of 3 is 9.

11. No homework is fun. Reading is homework. Reading is not fun. What type of argument is this?

    a. Deductive

    b. Inductive

12. The interior angles of an equilateral triangle are equal and the side lengths are equal.

Conjecture: Shapes having equal interior angles have equal side lengths.

Which of the following is a counterexample for the given conjecture?

    a. A square

    b. A regular hexagon

    c. Rectangle

    d. Trapezoid

13. What is the inverse of the conditional statement "If two angles are supplementary, then their sum is $180°$?"

    a. If two angles are not supplementary, then their sum is not $180°$.

    b. If the sum of two angles is $180°$, then they are supplementary angles.

    c. If two angles are supplementary, then their sum is not $180°$.

    d. If the sum of two angles is not $180°$, then they are not supplementary angles.

14. Providing a direct proof, decide which of the following is incorrect.

    a. If $a = b$ and $b = c$, then $a = c$.

    b. If 3^a is odd, then a is odd.

    c. If b^3 is even, then b is even.

    d. If $2^{a*b} < 16$, then $a * b < 4$.

Skills and Competencies

Part I - Algebra

1. Rewrite expressions with radical and rational numbers

2. Perform operations with complex numbers

3. Operations on matrices

4. Perform operations with quadratics

5. Solve equations with rational or radical expressions

6. Perform operations with quadratics

7. Identify graphs of linear equations or inequality with 2 variables on coordinate plane

8. Solve word problems with quadratics

9. Perform operations with quadratics

10. Perform operations with polynomials

11. Perform operations with polynomials

12. Solve problems with graphs of quadratics

13. Identify the equation of line that is perpendicular or parallel to a given line

14. Solve systems of linear equations in 2 variables

15. Solve quadratic word problems

16. Solve quadratic word problems

17. Determine the slope of a line

18. Solve quadratic word problems

19. Real world problems with ratio, proportion,

20. Simplify and approximate radicals

Part II - Functions

1. Describe the behavior of functions

2. Determine the first derivative of a function

3. Calculate antiderivatives

4. Solve problems with arithmetic sequences

5. Perform operations with functions

6. Perform operations with functions

7. Calculate inverse functions

8. Calculate inverse functions

9. Perform operations with functions

10. Determine the domain and range of a given table of values

Part III - Geometry

1. Solve problems with Pythagorean geometry

2. Determine congruence

3. Reflect geometric shapes

4. Calculate the perimeter of geometric shapes

5. Calculate the distance between two points

6. Determine interior angles

7. Determine congruence

8. Apply theorems to determine secants

9. Apply theorems to determine the radius of a circle.

10. Apply formulas to calculate the volume of a cone

11. Determine the directrix, given appropriate information.

12. Determine the coordinates of a circle, given appropriate information.

13. Reflect geometric shapes

14. Solve problems with Pythagorean geometry

15. Reflect geometric shapes

Part IV - Trigonometry

1. Determine equations of graphs or circular / trigonometric functions and their inverse.

2. Prove circular / trigonometric function identities or apply them to solve problems

3. Analyze graphs of trigonometric functions (period)

4. Solve real-world problems involving triangles using the law of sines or the law of cosines

5. Apply trigonometric equations to solve right triangle problems

Part V - Calculus

6. Interpret derivatives and definite integrals as limits (difference quotients, slope, Riemann sums area)

7. Determine limits using theorems concerning quotients of functions

8. Determine the slope or equation of a tangent line at a point on a curve

9. Use the Determine the first derivative of a function in various representations to determine increasing and decreasing intervals or extrema

10. Use the second derivative of a given function in various representations to determine intervals of concavity or points of inflection

Part VI - Statistics and Probability

1. Probability with dependent values

2. Independence and conditional probability

3. Analyze and interpret types of data - histogram

4. Interpret data on two categorical and quantitative variables (e.g., correlation, linear regression, two-way tables) or identify an appropriate representation

5. Identify the processes used to design and conduct statistical experiments including possible sources of bias

6. Calculate weighted scores

7. Solve problems using the Fundamental Counting Principle, permutations, and combinations

Part VII - Mathematical Reasoning

8. Identify and compare the contrapositive of a conditional statement.

9. Analyze mathematical assertions with proofs.

10. Identify examples of inductive reasoning.

11. Identify examples of deductive reasoning

12. Evaluate arguments or conjectures using laws of logic or counterexamples

13. Identify or compare the converse, inverse, and contrapositive of a conditional statement

14. Analyze mathematical assertions within proofs

Answer Key

Part I - Algebra

1. A
Here, we see that the numbers inside the roots are not prime numbers, so we may find perfect square multipliers inside these numbers. Then, we can take these numbers out of the root as factors:

$\sqrt{75} + \sqrt{48} - \sqrt{3 / 0.01} = \sqrt{3.25} + \sqrt{3.16} - \sqrt{3 / 0.01}$

$= \sqrt{3.5^2} + \sqrt{3.4^2} - \sqrt{3 / 0.1^2}$

$= 5\sqrt{3} + 4\sqrt{3} - (1/0.1)\sqrt{3}$

Here, notice that $1/0.1 = 10/1 = 10$:

$= (5 + 4 - 10)\sqrt{3}$

$= -\sqrt{3}$

2. B
In this type of questions, it is essential to recall that $i^2 = -1$.

We are given that $x = a + bi$ and $y = a - bi$. To find $x * y$, we need to multiply these two expressions:

$x * y = (a + bi)(a - bi) = a^2 - abi + abi - b^2i^2 = a^2 + b^2$
So, $x.y = a^2 + b^2 = 5a^2$
Then, $b^2 = 4a^2$

To obtain b alone, take the square root of both sides:
$\sqrt{b^2} = \sqrt{4a^2}$

b = 2a and b = - 2a
There are two possible solutions for b: 2a and -2a. We only find 2a in the answer choices.

3. B
Find the determinant of a matrix using the formula:
$$\det A = a_{11}\det A_{11} - a_{12}\det A_{12} + a_{13}\det A_{13} - \ldots + (-1)^{1+n} a_{1n}\det A_{1n}$$

$$= \sum_{j=1}^{n}(-1)^{1+j}\, a_{1j}\det A_{1j}$$

Here, A_{1j} named matrices are the submatrices obtained by closing 1st row and column j in the matrix A. The closed row and column elements are eliminated and the remaining entries form A_{1j} submatrices. The determinant of a 2x2 matrix is obtained by:

If A = $\begin{bmatrix} a & b \\ c & d \end{bmatrix}$,   det A = ab - cd.

So, in this question:

$$\det A = \begin{bmatrix} 2 & -1 & 0 \\ 5 & 3 & 1 \\ 1 & 1 & -2 \end{bmatrix}$$

$$= 2\begin{bmatrix} 3 & 1 \\ 1 & -2 \end{bmatrix} -(-1)\begin{bmatrix} 5 & 1 \\ 1 & -2 \end{bmatrix} +0\begin{bmatrix} 5 & 3 \\ 1 & 1 \end{bmatrix}$$

$$= 2\,(3(-2) - 1\cdot1) + 1(5(-2) - 1\cdot1) + 0(5\cdot1 - 3\cdot1)$$
$$= 2(-7) + (-11) + 0$$
$$= -14 - 11$$
$$= -25$$

4. A
We need to find the greatest common divisor of the two

terms to factor the expression. We should remember that if the bases of the exponents is the same, the product is found by summing the powers and writing on the same base. Similarly; when dividing, the power of the divisor is subtracted from the power of the divided.

Both x^3y^3 and x^2y^8 contain x^2 and y^3. So,

$x^3y^3 - x^2y^8 = x * x^2y^3 - y^5 * x^2y^3$ ... We can take x^2y^3 out as the factor:

$= x^2y^3(x - y^5)$

5. A
Notice that the denominator of A and numerator of B; numerator of A and denominator of B are conjugates. If we equate the denominators of both A and B at the same number; it is easier to write A in terms of B.

$A = (\sqrt{3} - 1) / (\sqrt{5} + 1)$ $_{(\sqrt{3} + 1)}$

$= ((\sqrt{3} - 1) * (\sqrt{3} + 1)) / ((\sqrt{5} + 1) * (\sqrt{3} + 1)) = (3 - 1) / ((\sqrt{5} + 1) * (\sqrt{3} + 1))$

$= 2 / ((\sqrt{5} + 1) * (\sqrt{3} + 1))$

$B = (\sqrt{5} - 1) / (\sqrt{3} + 1)$ $_{(\sqrt{5} + 1)}$

$= ((\sqrt{5} - 1) * (\sqrt{5} + 1)) / ((\sqrt{5} + 1) * (\sqrt{3} + 1))$

$= (5 - 1) / ((\sqrt{5} + 1) * (\sqrt{3} + 1))$

$= 4 / ((\sqrt{5} + 1) * (\sqrt{3} + 1))$

There is no need to expand the denominators of the new forms of A and B since they are the same. Comparing the numerators is sufficient. Notice that B is 2 times A. So, A = B/2.

6. B
Solve $x^2 - 5x - 6 = 0$ using the factoring method.

We try to separate the middle term -5x to find common factors with x^2 and -6 separately:

$x^2 - 6x + x - 6 = 0$ ... Here, we see that x is a common factor for x^2 and -6x:

$x(x - 6) + x - 6 = 0$ ... Here, we have x times x - 6 and 1 time x - 6 summed up. This means that we have x + 1 times x - 6:

$(x + 1)(x - 6) = 0$ ... This is true when either or both of the expressions in the parenthesis are equal to zero:

x + 1 = 0 ... x = -1

x - 6 = 0 ... x = 6

-1 and 6 are the solutions for this quadratic equation.

7. A

By simple graphing, we can determine the shape in between the function and the axis. First, find the axis intersects of $y \leq 2x + 6$:

y = 2x + 6

x = 0 → y = 6

y = 0 → x = - 3

So, the linear function passes through coordinates (0, 6) and (- 3, 0). Checking if (0, 0) is within the function or not;

$y \leq 2x + 6$

$0 \leq 2 * 0 + 6$

$0 \leq 6$

we see that it is, so we shade the region containing the origin. The dark shaded region is the triangular shape that lies between the function y, x-xis and y-axis

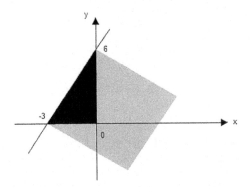

This is a triangle with an area found by half the base multiplied by height. The height is 6 units and the base is 3 units:

A = (3 * 6) / 2 = 9 units²

8. B
There are two statements made. This means that we can write two equations according to these statements:
The sum of two numbers are 21: x + y = 21

The sum of the squares is 261: x² + y² = 261

We are asked to find x and y.

Since we have the sums of the numbers and the sums of their squares; we can use the square formula of x + y, that is:

(x + y)² = x² + 2xy + y² ... Here, we can insert the known values x + y and x² + y²:

(21)² = 261 + 2xy ... Arranging to find xy:

441 = 261 + 2xy

441 - 261 = 2xy

180 = 2xy

xy = 180/2

xy = 90

We need to find two numbers which multiply to 90. Checking the answer choices, we see that in (b), 15 and 6 are given. 15 * 6 = 90. Also their squares sum up to 261 ($15^2 + 6^2 = 225 + 36 = 261$). So these two numbers satisfy the equation.

9. D
$x^2 + 4x + 4 = 0$ ... We try to separate the middle term 4x to find common factors with x^2 and 4 separately:

$x^2 + 2x + 2x + 4 = 0$ ... Here, we see that x is a common factor for x^2 and 2x, and 2 is a common factor for 2x and 4:

$x(x + 2) + 2(x + 2) = 0$ ... Here, we have x times x + 2 and 2 times x + 2 summed up. This means that we have x + 2 times x + 2:

$(x + 2)(x + 2) = 0$

$(x + 2)^2 = 0$ ... This is true if only if x + 2 is equal to zero.

x + 2 = 0

x = -2

10. A
Write in standard form $(3y^5 + y^4 + 2y^3 - 2y + 5) + (2y^5 + 3y^3 + 7y + 2)$
Arrange in columns of like terms and then add

$3y^5 + y^4 + 2y^3 - 2y + 5$
$2y^5 + 3y^3 + 7y + 2$

$5y^5 + y^4 + 5y^3 + 5y + 7$

11. B
$(x^2 - 2)(3x^2 - 3x + 7) = ?$

$= x^2(3x^2 - 3x + 7) - 2(3x^2 - 3x + 7)$

$= x^2(3x^2) + x^2(- 3x) + x \, 2(7) - 2(3x^2) - 2(-3x) - 2(7)$ (6 terms)

$= 3x^4 - 3x^3 + 7x^2 - 6x^2 + 6x - 14$

$= 3x^4 - 3x^3 + (7 - 6)x^2 + 6x - 14$

$= 3x^4 - 3x^3 + x^2 + 6x - 14$

12. B

Finding the x-intercepts of a function means that we need to equate the function to zero and find the roots of the equation:

$(x - 5)^2 - 9 = 9$

$(x - 5)^2 = 9$

$\sqrt{(x - 5)^2} = \sqrt{9}$

$x - 5 = 3 \rightarrow x = 8$

$x - 5 = -3 \rightarrow x = 2$

13. B

Recall that if two lines are parallel, they have the same slope. If we have an equation in the form of $y = mx + b$; m represents the slope of the line. The slope of line $y = \text{3x + 2 is 3. So, we are}$ searching for the choice that contains a slope value that is <u>not</u> 3:

    a. $3y = 9x - 8 \rightarrow y = 3x - 8/3 \rightarrow m = 3$
    b. $y = -2x + 2 \rightarrow m = -2$; This slope is not equal to 3.
    c. $y = 3x + 5 \rightarrow m = 3$
    d. $-4y = 5 - 12x \rightarrow 4y = 12x - 5 \rightarrow y = 3x - 5/4 \rightarrow m = 3$

14. C

First, we need to write two equations separately:

$4x - y = 5$ (I)

$x + 2y = 8$ (II) ... Here, we can use two ways to solve the system. One is substitution method, the other one is linear elimination method:

1. Substitution Method:

Equation (I) gives us that $y = 4x - 5$. We insert this value of y into equation (II):

$x + 2(4x - 5) = 8$

$x + 8x - 10 = 8$

$9x - 10 = 8$

$9x = 18$

x = 2

By knowing x = 2, we can find the value of y by inserting x = 2 into either of the equations. Choose equation (I):

4(2) - y = 5

8 - y = 5

8 - 5 = y

y = 3 → solution is (2, 3)

2. Linear Elimination Method:

2•/ 4x - y = 5 ... by multiplying equation (I) by 2, we see that -2y will form; and y terms

    x + 2y = 8 ... will be eliminated when summed with +2y in equation (II):

2•/ 4x - y = 5

+   x + 2y = 8

    8x - 2y = 10

  + x + 2y = 8 ... Summing side-by-side:

8x + x - 2y + 2y = 10 + 8 ... -2y and +2y cancel

9x = 18

x = 2

By knowing x = 2, we can find the value of y by inserting x = 2 into either of the equations. Choose equation (I):

4(2) - y = 5

8 - y = 5

8 - 5 = y

y = 3 → solution is (2, 3)

15. A
Two pieces of information are given, which can be translated

into two equations:

$x - y = 11 \rightarrow x = 11 + y$

$xy = 24$

$(11+y)y = -24$

$11y + y^2 = -24$

$y^2 + 11y + 24 = 0$

$y_{1,2} = (-11 \pm \sqrt{121 - 96})/2$

$y_{1,2} = (-11 \pm \sqrt{25})/2$

$y_{1,2} = (-11 \pm 5)/2$

$y_1 = -8$

$y_2 = -3$

$x_1 = 11 + y_1 = 11 - 8 = 3$

$x_2 = 11 + y_2 = 11 - 3 = 8$

16. C

x

$y = x + 1$

$z = x + 2$

$x^2 + y^2 = z^2$

$x^2 + (x + 1)^2 = (x + 2)^2$

$x^2 + x^2 + 2x + 1 = x^2 + 4x + 4$

$x^2 - 2x - 3 = 0$

$x_{1,2} = (2 \pm \sqrt{4 + 12})/2$

$x_{1,2} = (2 \pm 4)/2$

x = 3
y = 4
z = 5

17. C
Slope (m) = change in y
change in x

$(x_1, y_1) = (-3,1)$ & $(x_2, y_2) = (1,-4)$

Slope = [-4 - 1] / [1- (-3)] = -5/4

18. C
We are told that driver B is 20 km/h faster than driver A. So: $V_B = V_A + 20$ where V is the velocity. Also, driver B travelled 480 km 2 hours before driver A. So:

x = 480 km

$t_A - 2 = t_B$ where t is the time. Now we know the relationship between drivers A and B in terms of time and velocity. We need to write an equation only depending on V_A (the speed of driver A) which we are asked to find.

Since distance = velocity * time: $480 = V_A * t_A = V_B * t_B$

$480 = (V_A + 20)(t_A - 2)$

$480 = (V_A + 20) (480/ V_A - 2)$

$480 = 480 - 2V_A + 20 * 480/ V_A - 40$

$0 = -2V_A + 9600/ V_A - 40$ ... Multiplying the equation by V_A eliminates the denominator:

$2V_A^2 + 40V_A - 9600 = 0$ ... Simplifying the equation by 2:

$V_A^2 + 20V_A - 4800 = 0$

$V_{A\,1,2} = [- 20 \pm \sqrt{(400 + 4 * 4800)}] / 2$

$V_{A1,2} = [- 20 \pm 140] / 2$

$V_A = [-20 - 140]/2 = -80$ km/h and $V_A = [-20 + 140]/2$ = 60 km/h

We need to check our answers. It is easy to make a table:

t_A	V_A	V_B	t_B	$t_A - t_B$
480/80 = 6	-80	-80 - 20 = -100 B is 20 km/h faster than A. - sign only mentions the direction of the velocity. For magnitude, we need to add -20.	480/100 = 4.8	6 - 4.8 = 1.2 **This should be 2!**
480/60 = 8	60	60 + 20 = 80	480/80 = 6	8 - 6 = 2 **This is correct !**

So, $V_A = 60$ km/h is the only answer satisfying the question.

19. B
The total volume of the pool is 7V * 1/5 of the pool is 7V/5.
We need to set a simple ratio to find the result:
If the tap pours out y/4 liters of water per 1 minute

it pours out 7V/5 liters of water per x minutes

Here, we need to find x. Cross multiply the values:

y/4 liters → 1 minute

7V/5 liters → x minutes

x * y/4 = 7V / 5

x = (7V/5) / (y/4) = (7v/5) * (4/y)

x = 28V/5y

20. A

First, insert the values of x and y into the expression given:
$(x + y) / (x - y) = (\sqrt{7} - 1 + \sqrt{7} + 1) / (\sqrt{7} - 1 - (\sqrt{7} + 1))$

$= (2\sqrt{7}) / (\sqrt{7} - 1 - \sqrt{7} - 1) = (2\sqrt{7}) / (- 2) = - \sqrt{7}$

Part II - Functions

1. D

Drawing the graph of a 5th degree polynomial is not a practical way to solve this problem. Instead; we need to remember some properties of polynomial graphs:

Notice that this is an odd degree polynomial. So, two ends of the graph head off in opposite directions. If the leading term is positive; the left end would be down and the right end would be up. However, the leading term here is $-2x^5$ that is negative. So, the end behavior for this function is up on the left and down on the right.

2. B

We are asked to find the first derivative of function f that is the multiplication of functions g and h:

$f(x) = (x^2 - 2)(x^2 - 2)^3 = (x^2 - 2)^4$

The simple derivation formula of exponential expressions is: $(d/dx)\, x^n = n * x^{n-1}$. However, in this question, the function that is the base of the exponential is a function of x. The general formula should be applied for derivation is:

$(d/dx)\, [a(x)^n] = n * a(x)^{n-1} * a\,'(x)$

$(d/dx)\, [(x^2 - 2)^4] = 4 * (x^2 - 2)^3 * (2x)$

$= 8x(x^2 - 3)^3$

3. C

The antiderivative of a function f, is the function that when derived, f is obtained. We can find the antiderivative of each term separately and then combine:

The antiderivative of $1/x$ is $\int dx/x = \ln x + C_1$

The antiderivative of x^3 is $\int x^3 \, dx = x^4/4 + C_2$

The antiderivative of cosx is $\int \cos x \, dx = \sin x + C_3$

The overall antiderivative of the expression $1/x + x^3 - \cos x$ is:

$\int (1/x + x^3 - \cos x) \, dx = \ln x + x^4/4 - \sin x + C$ when all constants are collected under "C."

4. D
We know that $a_n = 7^{2n-5}$. Calculate a_{n+2}:

$a_{n+2} = 7^{2(n+2) - 5} = 7^{2n+4-5} = 7^4 * 7^{2n-5} = 7^4 * a_n$

7^4 times a_n is equal to a_{n+2}.

5. B
Following the parts of the piecewise function, find the values of the given functions by inserting the x values into the corresponding definition:

$x = 1 \rightarrow f(x) = -x/2 \rightarrow f(1) = -1/2$

$x = 3 \rightarrow f(x) = x^3 + 2 \rightarrow f(3) = 3^3 + 2 = 29$

$x = 0 \rightarrow f(x) = -x/2 \rightarrow f(0) = 0$

$x = 2 \rightarrow f(x) = x^3 + 2 \rightarrow f(2) = 2^3 + 2 = 10$

$(f(1) * f(3) - f(0)) / f^2(2) = (-1/2 * 29 - 0) / 10^2 = -29/200 = -0.145$

6. B
$f(x) = -x$

$g(x) = 2x + 1$

$h(x) = x^2$

$f \circ g \circ h = f(g(h(x)))$

$= f(g(x^2))$

$= f(2x^2 + 1)$

$= -(2x^2 + 1)$

$= -2x^2 - 1$

7. D
$f(x) = 3x + 3$

$f^{-1}(f(x)) = x$

$f^{-1}(3x + 3) = x$

$3x + 3 = t$

$3x = t - 3$

$x = (t - 3)/3$

$f^{-1}(t) = (t - 3)/3$

$f^{-1}(x) = (x - 3)/3$

8. C
$f(x) = (5x - 2)/4$

$f^{-1}(f(x)) = x$

$f^{-1}((5x - 2)/4) = x$

$(5x - 2)/4 = t$

$5x - 2 = 4t$

$5x = 4t + 2$

$x = (4t + 2)/5$

$f^{-1}(t) = (4t + 2)/5$

$f^{-1}(x) = (4x + 2)/5$

9. B

$f(x) = 1 - x$

$f^{-1}(1 - x) = x$

$1 - x = t$

$x = 1 - t$

$f^{-1}(t) = 1 - t$

$f^{-1}(x) = 1 - x$

$f^{-1}(1/2) = 1 - 1/2 = 1/2$

10. C

The x values are the domain and the y values are the range. The domain of this set of data is {-5, 2, 4, 7, 12} and the range is {-3, 4, 9, 15, 18}.

Part III - Geometry

1. B

There are three squares forming a right triangle in the middle. Two of the squares have the areas 81 m² and 144 m². Denote their sides a and b respectively:

$a^2 = 81$ and $b^2 = 144$. The length, which is asked, is the hypotenuse; a and b are the opposite and adjacent sides of the right angle. Using the Pythagorean Theorem, we can find the value of the side:

Pythagorean Theorem:

$(\text{Hypotenuse})^2 = (\text{Opposite Side})^2 + (\text{Adjacent Side})^2$

$h^2 = a^2 + b^2$

$a^2 = 81$ and $b^2 = 144$ are given. So,

$h^2 = 81 + 144$

$h^2 = 225$

h = 15 m

2. A
Yes, the triangles are congruence - a case of SSA:

3.
We reflect the center O against the mirror line m at right angle and we use a compass to draw the circle with the same radius as the original circle.

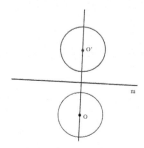

4. A
The question is to find the perimeter of a shape made by merging a square and a semi circle. Perimeter = 3 sides of the square + ½ circumference of the circle.

= (3 x 5) + ½(5 π)
= 15 + 2.5 π
Perimeter = 22.85 cm

5. D
The distance between two points is found by
$[(x_2 - x_1)^2 + (y_2 - y_1)^2]^{1/2}$

In this question:

(18, 12) : x_1 = 18, y_1 = 12

(9, -6) : x_2 = 9, y_2 = -6

Distance= $[(9 - 18)^2 + (-6 - 12)^2]^{1/2}$

$= [(-9)^2 + (-18)^2]^{1/2}$

$= (9^2 + 2^2 * 9^2)^{1/2}$

$= (9^2(1 + 4))^{1/2}$ ... We can take 9 out of the square root:

$= 9 * 5^{1/2}$

$= 9\sqrt{5}$

$= 9 * 2.45$

$= 20.12$

The distance is about 22 units.

6. D
Two parallel lines(m & side AB) intersected by side AC
a = 50° (interior angles).

7. A
This is a case of ASA:

So the 2 triangles are congruent

8. D
If any two secants intersect at a point as above, there is the below relationship between the segments:
|AN| * |NC| = |BN| * |ND|

So:

2 * 14 = 4 * x

x = 7

9. D

Remember that a peripheral angle that is 90⁰, sees the diameter of the circle. Also, the tangents with the same starting point have the same lengths and the line connecting the center of the circle to the tangent points are perpendicular to the tangent lines as shown below:

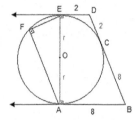

With simple geometry, we can find the value of r:

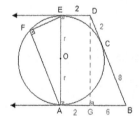

In triangle DGB, apply the Pythagorean Theorem:

$(2r)^2 + 6^2 = (2 + 8)^2$

$4r^2 + 36 = 100$

$4r^2 = 64 \rightarrow r^2 = 16 \rightarrow r = 4$ cm

10. C

The volume of a cone is 1/3 of the volume of a cylinder of the same height:

$V = (\pi r^2 h) / 3$

where r: radius, h: height. Insert the given values:

$V = (\pi r^2 h) / 3 = (\pi * 5^2 * 12) / 3 = 100\pi$ cm^3 $= 100\pi * 10^{-6}$ m^3

$= \pi * 10^{-4}$ m^3

11. D

Recall that the formula including the focus (a, b) and directrix (y = k) information is in the form:

$$y = (1/(2(b - k))) * (x - a)^2 + (b + k)/2$$

We need to re-organise the given equation to find the value of k:

$$y - 5/2 = (-1/2)(x - 2)^2$$

$$y = (-1/2)(x - 2)^2 + 5/2$$

So,

$$a = 2$$

$$1 / (2(b - k)) = -1/2 \rightarrow b - k = -1 \dots \text{(I)}$$

$$(b + k) / 2 = 5/2 \rightarrow b + k = 5 \dots \text{(II)}$$

Using the equations (I) and (II) and by eliminating b, we can find the value of k that is the directrix:

$$- / \ b - k = - 1$$

$$\underline{b + k = 5}$$

$$2k = 6$$

$$k = 3$$

12. B

The general form of circle equations is as follows:

$$(x - a)^2 + (y - b)^2 = r^2$$ where (a, b) gives the center coordinates and r is the radius.

We are asked to find (a, b); therefore, we need to reorganize the given equation to obtain the form above:

$$x^2 + y^2 - 6x + 4y + 4 = 0$$

$$x^2 - 6x + y^2 + 4y = - 4$$

$$x^2 - 6x + \nabla + y^2 + 4y + \Diamond = - 4 + \nabla + \Diamond$$

We need to find the appropriate values for the symbols ∇ and ◊ to obtain perfect squares. Note that -6x and + 4y are the 2ab terms in the expansion $(a ± b)^2 = a^2 ± 2ab + b^2$. Then;

x^2 - 6x + ∇ + y^2 + 4y + ◊ = -4 + ∇ + ◊

x^2 - 6x + <u>9</u> + y^2 + 4y + <u>4</u> = -4 + <u>9</u> + <u>4</u>

$(x - 3)^2 + (y + 2)^2 = 9$

So, the center of the circle is (3, -2).

13. A
Observe that this is a right triangle and is on the x-axis. When this is reflected across the x-axis; the following shape is obtained:

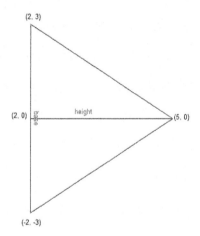

This means that the area is doubled. The area of this compound triangle is found by:

(height * base)/2 = (|5 - 2| * |3 - (-2)|) / 2

= 9 units²

14. B
In the question, we have a right triangle formed inside the circle. We are asked to find the length of the hypotenuse of this triangle. We can find the other two sides of the triangle by using the properties of a circle.

The diameter of the circle is equal to 12 cm. The legs of the right triangle are the radii of the circle; so they are 6 cm long.

Using the Pythagorean Theorem:

$(\text{Hypotenuse})^2 = (\text{Adjacent Side})^2 + (\text{Opposite Side})^2$

$x^2 = r^2 + r^2$

$x^2 = 6^2 + 6^2$

$x^2 = 72$

$x = \sqrt{72}$

$x = 8.48$

15.
We reflect points A, B, C and D against the mirror line m at right angle and we connect the new points A', B',C' and D'.

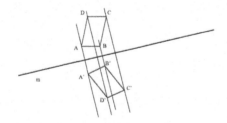

Part IV - Trigonometry

1. B
First denote,

$\arccos(1/5) = a$

$\arcsin(1/5) = b$

Then, we are asked to find $a + b$. Eliminate the inverses of the trigonometric functions:

$\cos(\arccos(1/5)) = \cos a \rightarrow \cos a = 1/5$

$\sin(\arcsin(1/5)) = \sin b \rightarrow \sin b = 1/5$

We see that $\cos a = \sin b$. This is possible if only if $a + b = \pi/2$.

2. B
The properties used are:
$\tan x = \sin x / \cos x$, $\csc x = 1 / \sin x$, $\sin^2 x + \cos^2 x = 1$, $a^3 - b^3 = (a - b)(a^2 + ab + b^2)$

$(\tan x * \sin x - \cot x * \cos x) / (\cos x + \csc x) = ((\sin x / \cos x) * \sin x - (\cos x / \sin x) * \cos x) / (\cos x + 1 / \sin x)$

$= ((\sin^2 x / \cos x) - (\cos^2 x / \sin x)) / ((\sin x * \cos x + 1) / \sin x)$

$= ((\sin^3 x - \cos^3 x) / (\cos x * \sin x)) / ((\sin x * \cos x + 1) / \sin x)$

$= ((\sin^3 x - \cos^3 x) / (\cos x * \sin x)) * (\sin x / (\sin x * \cos x + 1))$

$= ((\sin x - \cos x)(\sin^2 x + \sin x * \cos x + \cos^2 x) / (\cos x * \sin x)) * (\sin x / (\sin x * \cos x + 1))$
$= ((\sin x - \cos x)(1 + \sin x * \cos x) / (\cos x * \sin x)) * (\sin x / (\sin x * \cos x + 1))$

$= (\sin x - \cos x) / \cos x$

$= \sin x / \cos x - 1$

$= \tan x - 1$

3. B
Period is the duration between two cases when the movement is in the same direction passing through the same point:

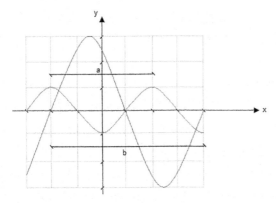

The period for a = 4 units

The period for b = 6 units

|b - a| = |6 - 4| = 2 units

4. B
Here, we need to apply the Law of Sine since we know two angles of the triangle and one side length:

a / sinA = b / sinB = c / sinC

Inserting the known values,

5/ sin60 = b / sin40 = c / sin(180 - (60 + 40))

5/ (√3 / 2) = b / sin40 = c / sin80

10 / √3 = b / sin40   b = 3.711 m

10 / √3 = c / sin80   c = 5.686 m

|b - c| = |3.711 - 5.686| = 1.975 m

5. D
Remember that the area of a triangle is half the product of its height and base. Here, there are several ways to find the solution. However, we are asked to use trigonometric functions which means that we use trigonometric functions to find the height perpendicular to the side with 10 units:

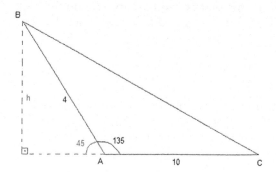

Notice that h = 4 * sin45 = 4√2 / 2 = 2√2. Then, the area of the triangle is:

A = (h * 10) / 2 = 2√2 * 10 / 2 = 10√2 units²

Part VI - Calculus

6. C
Expand the given expression:

$$\int_{-1}^{3}(4g(x) - 5f(x))dx = \int_{-1}^{3}4g(x)dx - \int_{-1}^{3}5f(x))dx$$

Notice that the limits of the integrals change from - 1 to 3. In the given integrals, they change from - 1 to 3 for f(x), but from 3 to - 1 for g(x). We can do the following shifting:

$$\int_{3}^{-1}g(x)dx = 8 \rightarrow \int_{-1}^{3}g(x)dx = -8$$

So:

$$\int_{-1}^{3}4g(x)dx - \int_{-1}^{3}5f(x))dx = 4\int_{-1}^{3}g(x)dx - 5\int_{-1}^{3}f(x))dx$$

= 4(-8) - 5(-15) = -32 + 75 = 43

7. C

While dealing with limit problems, we first insert the limit of x into the function. If it contains indefinite cases, we carry on:

$$\lim_{x \to 5} (\tan(x^2 - 25) / (x - 5)) = \tan 0 / (5 - 5) = 0/0$$

Since this result is indefinite, we perform L'Hopital Rule. It says that in case we find $0/0$ or ∞/∞, we need to take the derivative of both numerator and denominator and then insert the limit of x:

$$\lim_{x \to 5} (\tan(x^2 - 25) / (x - 5))$$

$$= \lim_{x \to 5} (((d/dx) \tan(x^2 - 25)) / ((d/dx) (x - 5)))$$

$$= \lim_{x \to 5} (2x * \sec^2(x^2 - 25)) / 1 = 2 * 5 * \sec^2 0 = 10 * 1 = 10$$

8. D

The first order derivative of a function is equal to the slope of the tangent line. We are asked to find the slope of the formula:

$$y = 4\sqrt{x}$$

$$y' = 4 * (1/2) * x^{-1/2} = 2 / \sqrt{x}$$

at x = 2:

$$y' = 2 / \sqrt{2} = \sqrt{2} \ ... \text{This is the slope of line tangent to the}$$
curve.

9. C

First, find the first derivative of the function to understand where it is increasing and decreasing:

$$f(x) = (x + 4)^2$$

$$f'(x) = 2(x + 4) * 1 = 2(x + 4)$$

Second, find the x values that make f' zero:

$$2(x + 4) = 0$$

x = -4

Now, choose values that are smaller and bigger than -4:

-5 (smaller) and 0 (bigger). Plugging these values into f' will help us understand the characteristics of f:

f'(-5) = 2(-5 + 4) = -2

f' (0) = 2(0 + 4) = 8

f increases in the interval where f' is positive. So, it increases on (-4, +∞).

10. B
The inflection point is the point where concavity changes sign. In other words; concavity goes up to down or down to up around the inflection point.

Both on the left and right sides of x = 2.2, concavity is up.

On the left side of x = -1, concavity is up; however, it is down on the right side. So, this is an inflection point.

Both on the left and right sides of x = 1.5, concavity is down.

On the left side of x = 3, concavity is down; however, it is up on the right side. So, this is an inflection point.

Both on the left and right sides of x = 4.5, concavity is up.

We do not know the characteristics of the graph after x = 4.5.

So, the inflection points are -1 and 3.

Part V - Statistics and Probability

1. A
There are 8 balls in the bag in total. It is important that two balls are taken out of the bag one by one. We can first take the blue then the white, or first white, then the blue. So, we will have two possibilities to be summed up. Since the balls are taken consecutively, we should be careful with the total number of balls for each case:

First blue, then white ball:

There are 3 blue balls; so, having a blue ball is 3/8 possible. Then, we have 7 balls left in the bag. The possibility to have a white ball is 1/7.

P = (3/8) * (1/7) = 3/56

First white, then blue ball:

There is only 1 white ball; so, having a white ball is 1/8 possible. Then, we have 7 balls left in the bag. The possibility to have a blue ball is 3/7.

P = (1/8) * (3/7) = 3/56

Overall probability is:

3/56 + 3/56 = 3/28

2. D
Assume that the first book chosen is red. Since we need to choose the second book in green or blue, there are 10 possible books to be chosen out of 15 - 1(that is the red book chosen first) = 14 books. There are equal number of books in each color, so the results will be the same if we think that blue or green book is the first book.

So, the probability will be 10/14 = 5/7.

3. B
Reading the data on the histogram, we see that 18 students got 62 points. The total number of students is:

2 + 8 + 12 + 20 + 34 + 40 + 18 + 14 + 8 + 2 = 158

The frequency density of 18 students is:

18/158 = 0.114

4. D
In city A, 68% of the residents have no or 1 child. Since the total population is about 2 million; 1.36 million residents of city A have no, or 1 child.

In city B, 57% of the residents have no, or 1 child. Since the total population is approximately 4 million; 2.28 million residents of city B have no, or 1 child.

In total: 1.36 + 2.28 = 3.64 million residents have no, or 1 child.

5. C
The ones in the front row are more likely to follow the lessons and be successful compared to the ones behind, because they can listen more carefully. So, weaker members are eliminated from the sample. That is why, survivorship bias is observed in this sampling.

6. C
Calculate the weighted score by taking the sum of the products of scores and credits of each course divided by total number of credits:

$\bar{x}$ = (2 * 3 + 3 * 2*5 + 4 * 4 + 1 * 1*5 + 1 * 2*5 + 4 * 3*5 + 5 * 3) / (2 + 3 + 4 + 1 + 1 + 4 + 5)

= 3.125

7. C
We are asked to order 10 books on a shelf in total. However, there is a limitation; we cannot separate the books of the same category. That is why we need to think two points: The books of the same category can be ordered in different ways and chemistry books, physics books and mathematics books as three huge books can be ordered in different ways.

Chemistry books can be ordered in 3! different ways

Physics books can be ordered in 2! different ways

Mathematics books can be ordered in 5! different ways

Three huge books can be ordered in 3! different ways

Overall; these books can be ordered in 2! * 3! * 3! * 5! different ways.

Part VII - Mathematical Reasoning

8. A

The conditional statement is given as "If 3 times a equals 12, then a is an integer."

Here, we need to identify the hypothesis and the conclusion. The hypothesis (p) is "3 times a equal 12" and the conclusion is (q) "a is an integer." We say that $p \rightarrow q$.

The contrapositive statement is written as $\sim q \rightarrow \sim p$, where the '$\sim$' sign means "not."

$\sim q$ is: a is <u>not</u> an integer.

$\sim p$ is: 3 times a <u>does not</u> equal 12.

So, the contrapositive statement is: If a is not an integer, then 3 time a does not equal 12.

9. A

Consider each choice:

a. For all integers n; if n is odd, then n^2 is odd. This assertion is true, there is no odd integer of which square is even. The converse of this assertion is: For all integers n; if n^2 is odd, then n is odd. This is true as well, because there is no even n^2 providing that n is odd. So, both the conditional assertion and its converse have the same truth value.

b. For all real numbers a; if a < 0, then a < 5. This assertion is true, there is no real number less than 0 that is higher than 5 at the same time. The converse of this assertion is: For all real numbers a; if a < 5, then a < 0. This is false, for example 4 is smaller than 5 but is not smaller than 0 at the same time. So, the conditional assertion and its converse do not have the same truth value.

c. If it is a cat, then it has whiskers. This assertion is true; cats have whiskers, unless there is a special case (genetic modification, maybe). The converse of this assertion is: If it has whiskers, then it is a cat. This is false, not only cats have whiskers; dogs, sea lions,

lions, pumas…etc. also have. So, the conditional assertion and its converse do not have the same truth value.

d. If a number is divisible by 25, then it is divisible by
5. This assertion is true; if a number contains 25 as a
factor, then it contains two 5s which means that it is
divisible by 5 as well. The converse of this assertion is:
If a number is divisible by 5, then it is divisible by 25.
This is false, for example 30 is divisible by 5, but is not
divisible by 25. So, the conditional assertion and its
converse do not have the same truth value.

10. A
Inductive reasoning is to derive a general rule from a specific case. Only choice A, "My dog barks. The dogs I see in
our neighborhood barks. Therefore, every dog barks" is an
example inductive reasoning. The barking property of my
dog and the dogs in my neighborhood result in the rule that
every dog barks.

Examining the other choices:

> **b.** Quadrilaterals have four sides is a general rule.
> Square is a special quadrilateral and to say that it has
> four sides is deductive reasoning.

> **c.** The general information is that all the apples on the
> tree are red. Proceeding from this, it is deducted that
> the apple randomly chosen from the tree is red.

> **d.** It is a general rule to say that the square of a num-
> ber is found by multiplying the number by itself. To
> say that the square of 3 is 9, is a specific case and is
> therefore deductive reasoning.

11. A
This is a very strong deductive argument. If the first two
statement are true, then the third statement or conclusion
must be true.

12. C
The counterexample for the given conjecture should be an

example that disclaims the conjecture. So, we are searching for the shape that has equal interior angles but non equal side lengths; or, the shape that has equal side lengths but non equal interior angles. The second is not possible to obtain since equal side lengths result in equal interior angles. A rectangle has equal interior angles of 90^0, but it has a width and a length; it is not an equilateral shape.

Also, a trapezoid does not have equal side-lengths but since it also does not have equal lengths, this shape is out of evaluation.

13. A

The conditional statement is given as "If two angles are supplementary, then their sum is 180^0." Here, we need to identify the hypothesis and the conclusion. The hypothesis (p) is "two angles are supplementary" and the conclusion is (q) "their sum is 180^0."

We say that $p \rightarrow q$.
The inverse statement is written as $\sim p \rightarrow \sim q$, where "$\sim$" means "not."

$\sim q$ is: their sum is <u>not</u> 180^0

$\sim p$ is: two angles are <u>not</u> supplementary

So, the inverse statement is: If two angles are not supplementary, then their sum is not 180^0.

14. B

Examining the choices, choice B is the only correct choice (i.e wrong):

a. Let us say that $a = k$. Then, since $a = b$, b is equal to k as well as a. So, c is also equal to k:

$a = k$
$b = k$
$c = k$

Then, $a = c$ is obtained. So, this is a correct statement.

b. If 3a is odd, let us say that 3a = 2k. Then, a = 2k/3. Here, a may be a decimal number as well as an odd or even number. However, we cannot say that a is odd. For example, if k = 1, then a will be 2/3 which is neither odd nor even. So, this is an incorrect statement.

c. Let us say that $b^3 = 2k$ that is an even number. Then, b = 3√(2k). The term inside the root should be the third power of a number so that it can go out of the root as an integer. Having a "2" factor inside; to complete to third order; k should contain the square of 2 inside. So, we can say that k = 4a. Since 4 is an even number and the result of its multiplication with any number is even, k is even as well. So, this is a correct statement.

d. 16 is the 4th degree of 2. Then; $16 = 2^4$. If $2^{a*b} < 16$, then $2^{a*b} < 24$. Since the bases are same; a * b should be smaller than 4. So, this is a correct statement.

Practice Test Questions Set 2

The questions below are not the same as you will find
on the FTCE Mathematics test- that would be too easy!
And nobody knows what the questions will be and they
change all the time. Below are general questions that cover
the same subject areas as the FTCE Mathematics test. So,
while the format and exact wording of the questions may differ slightly, and change from year to year, if you can answer
the questions below, you will have no problem with the FTCE
Mathematics test.

For the best results, take these Practice Test Questions as
if it were the real exam. Set aside time when you will not be
disturbed, and a location that is quiet and free of distractions. Read the instructions carefully, read each question
carefully, and answer to the best of your ability.
Use the bubble answer sheets provided. When you have
completed the Practice Questions, check your answer
against the Answer Key and read the explanation provided.

Do not attempt more than one set of practice test questions
in one day. After completing the first practice test, wait two
or three days before attempting the second set of questions.

Algebra Answer Sheet

1. (A) (B) (C) (D)   11. (A) (B) (C) (D)

2. (A) (B) (C) (D)   12. (A) (B) (C) (D)

3. (A) (B) (C) (D)   13. (A) (B) (C) (D)

4. (A) (B) (C) (D)   14. (A) (B) (C) (D)

5. (A) (B) (C) (D)   15. (A) (B) (C) (D)

6. (A) (B) (C) (D)   16. (A) (B) (C) (D)

7. (A) (B) (C) (D)   17. (A) (B) (C) (D)

8. (A) (B) (C) (D)   18. (A) (B) (C) (D)

9. (A) (B) (C) (D)   19. (A) (B) (C) (D)

10. (A) (B) (C) (D)   20. (A) (B) (C) (D)

Functions Answer Sheet

1. (A) (B) (C) (D)   11. (A) (B) (C) (D)

2. (A) (B) (C) (D)   12. (A) (B) (C) (D)

3. (A) (B) (C) (D)   13. (A) (B) (C) (D)

4. (A) (B) (C) (D)   14. (A) (B) (C) (D)

5. (A) (B) (C) (D)   15. (A) (B) (C) (D)

6. (A) (B) (C) (D)

7. (A) (B) (C) (D)

8. (A) (B) (C) (D)

9. (A) (B) (C) (D)

10. (A) (B) (C) (D)

Geometry Answer Sheet

1. (A) (B) (C) (D)   11. (A) (B) (C) (D)

2. (A) (B) (C) (D)   12. (A) (B) (C) (D)

3. (A) (B) (C) (D)   13. (A) (B) (C) (D)

4. (A) (B) (C) (D)   14. (A) (B) (C) (D)

5. (A) (B) (C) (D)   15. (A) (B) (C) (D)

6. (A) (B) (C) (D)

7. (A) (B) (C) (D)

8. (A) (B) (C) (D)

9. (A) (B) (C) (D)

10. (A) (B) (C) (D)

Trigonometry and Calculus Answer Sheet

1. (A) (B) (C) (D)

2. (A) (B) (C) (D)

3. (A) (B) (C) (D)

4. (A) (B) (C) (D)

5. (A) (B) (C) (D)

6. (A) (B) (C) (D)

7. (A) (B) (C) (D)

8. (A) (B) (C) (D)

9. (A) (B) (C) (D)

10. (A) (B) (C) (D)

Statistics Probability and Mathematical Reasoning Answer Sheet

1. Ⓐ Ⓑ Ⓒ Ⓓ   11. Ⓐ Ⓑ Ⓒ Ⓓ

2. Ⓐ Ⓑ Ⓒ Ⓓ   12. Ⓐ Ⓑ Ⓒ Ⓓ

3. Ⓐ Ⓑ Ⓒ Ⓓ   13. Ⓐ Ⓑ Ⓒ Ⓓ

4. Ⓐ Ⓑ Ⓒ Ⓓ   14. Ⓐ Ⓑ Ⓒ Ⓓ

5. Ⓐ Ⓑ Ⓒ Ⓓ   15. Ⓐ Ⓑ Ⓒ Ⓓ

6. Ⓐ Ⓑ Ⓒ Ⓓ

7. Ⓐ Ⓑ Ⓒ Ⓓ

8. Ⓐ Ⓑ Ⓒ Ⓓ

9. Ⓐ Ⓑ Ⓒ Ⓓ

10. Ⓐ Ⓑ Ⓒ Ⓓ

Part I - Algebra

1. Simplify the following expression in rational number form:

$(\sqrt{4/9} * 3/8) / ((\sqrt[3]{125} / \sqrt[4]{81}) / 4 - 1/12).$

    a. 1/2

    b. 3/4

    c. 4/3

    d. 2

2. What is the result of the expression
$(i^{18} - i^5 + 4i^{162} - i^{39}) / (i^2 - 1)$ **?**

    b. 2

    b. 5/2

    c. 7/2

    d. 5

3. We are given that A = $\begin{bmatrix} 1 & 4 \\ 1 & 3 \end{bmatrix}$ **and B =** $\begin{bmatrix} 2 & 2 \\ 5 & 1 \end{bmatrix}$

Find the X matrix that satisfies A * X = B.

a. $\begin{bmatrix} 4 & -2 \\ -3 & 0 \end{bmatrix}$ b. $\begin{bmatrix} 3 & -2 \\ -3 & 1 \end{bmatrix}$ c. $\begin{bmatrix} 2 & -2 \\ -3 & 3 \end{bmatrix}$ d. $\begin{bmatrix} 14 & -2 \\ -3 & 1 \end{bmatrix}$

4. Using the factoring method, solve the quadratic equation: $2x^2 - 3x = 0$

    a. 0 and 1.5

    b. 1.5 and 2

    c. 2 and 2.5

    d. 0 and 2

5. Using the quadratic formula, solve the quadratic equation: $x^2 - 9x + 14 = 0$

    a. 2 and 7

    b. -2 and 7

    c. -7 and -2

    d. -7 and 2

6. Factor the polynomial $9x^2 - 6x + 12$.

    a. $3(x^2 - 2x + 9)$

    b. $3(3x^2 - 3x + 4)$

    c. $9(x^2 - 3x + 3)$

    d. $3(3x^2 - 2x + 4)$

7. Factor the polynomial $x^3y^3 - x^2y^8$.

    a. $x^2y^3(x - y^5)$

    b. $x^3y^3(1 - y^5)$

    c. $x^2y^2(x - y^6)$

    d. $xy^3(x - y^5)$

8. $(3y^5 - 2y + y^4 + 2y^3 + 5) - (2y^5 + 3y^3 + 2 + 7y) =$

    a. $y^5 + y^4 - y^3 - 9y + 3$

    b. $y^5 + y^4 - y^3 - 7y + 2$

    c. $y^3 + y^4 - y^2 - 9y + 3$

    d. $y^2 + y^4 - 2y^3 - 3y + 3$

9. Add -3x² + 2x + 6 and -x² - x - 1.

    a. -2x² + x + 5

    b. -4x² + x + 5

    c. -2x² + 3x + 5

    d. -4x² + 3x + 5

10.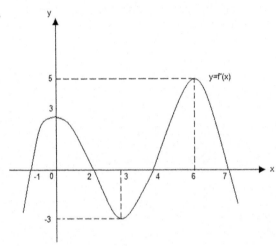

Graph of f "(x) is given above. Find the sum of apsides of vertexes of function f.

    a. 3

    b. 5

    c. 8

    d. 12

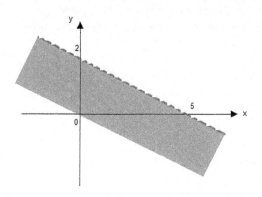

11. Which inequality represents the graph of the function above?

    a. y ≥ (- 2/5) x + 2
    b. y > (- 2/5) x + 2
    c. y < (- 2/5) x + 2
    d. y ≤ (- 2/5) x + 2

12. Find x and y from the following system of equations:

(4x + 5y)/3 = ((x - 3y)/2) + 4
(3x + y)/2 = ((2x + 7y)/3) -1

    a. (1, 3)
    b. (2, 1)
    c. (1, 1)
    d. (0, 1)

13. The area of a rectangle is 20 cm². If one side increases by 1 cm and other by 2 cm, the area of the new rectangle is 35 cm². Find the sides of the original rectangle.

  a. (4,8)

  b. (4,5)

  c. (2.5,8)

  d. b and c

14. Solve the linear equation:
   -x - 7 = -3x - 9

  a. -1

  b. 0

  c. 1

  d. 2

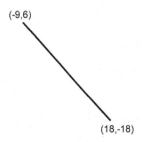

(-9,6)

(18,-18)

15. What is the slope of the line above?

  a. -8/9

  b. 9/8

  c. -9/8

  d. 8/9

16. 6 workers of the same capacity begin building a wall. Every day, one worker leaves, and the total job is completed in 4 days. If none of the workers left the job, how many days would it take to complete the wall?

   a. 1

   b. 1.5

   c. 2

   d. 3

17. Find the result of the operation ($\sqrt{75}$ - 3$\sqrt{48}$) / $\sqrt{147}$ + $\sqrt{20}$ by simplification and approximation and then rounding the result to tenths digit.

   a. - 4.4

   b. -3.4

   c. -2.8

   d. 3.2

18. $\sqrt[4]{(2 * \sqrt[3]{4})} * \sqrt[3]{\sqrt{8}} = \sqrt[6]{(4 * \sqrt[2]{2^{x+1}})}$ is given. Find the value of x.

   a. 2

   b. 3

   c. 5

   d. 6

19. ((1 - 1/3) * (1 + 1/5)) / (1/8 * 4/5 - 1/3) =

   a. -24/7

   b. -7/24

   c. 7/24

   d. 24/7

20. Simplify the expression $(a^3(4a)^{-2}b^8c) / (a^6(2a)^{-3}b^5c^{12})$.

    a. $(1/2)\ a^2b^6c^{-11}$

    b. $(1/8)\ a^{-2}b^3c^{-11}$

    c. $(1/2)\ a^{-2}b^3c^{-11}$

    d. $(1/2)\ a^{-2}b^{-3}c^{11}$

Part II - Functions

1. Find the domain of the function
$f(x) = \sqrt{(x + 7)} / (x - 3)$.

    a. $[3, 7) \cup (7, +\infty)$

    b. $(-\infty, 3) \cup (3, +\infty)$

    c. $[-7, 3) \cup (3, +\infty)$

    d. $[-7, 3) \cup (3, +\infty]$

2. Check if the given antiderivatives are correct for the given functions.

    1) $f(x) = x\ \sin 3x$
    antiderivative = $(-1/3)\ [x \cos 3x + (1/3) \sin 3x] + C$
    2) $f(x) = 1 / (2\sqrt{(3x^3)})$
    antiderivative = $-1 / \sqrt{(3x)} + C$

    a. 1) correct 2) incorrect

    b. 1) correct 2) correct

    c. 1) incorrect 2) incorrect

    d. 1) incorrect 2) correct

3. $\{a_n\} = \{2, 4, 6, ...\}$ and $\{b_n\} = \{4, 9, 14, ...\}$ are arithmetic sequences, each with 50 terms. How many common terms do these two sequences have?

    a. 4

    b. 6

    c. 8

    d. 10

4. After finding the first derivative of the function f(x) = (x³ + 1) / (x - 2), find the <u>remainder of the polynomial</u> division operation.

$$\frac{g(x)}{h(x)} = \frac{d(g(x)) \cdot h - d(h) \cdot g}{h^2}$$

    a. -9

    b. x + 1

    c. 10

    d. x - 1

5. There are two candles of the same length; one lasts for 2 hours and the other, 3 hours. After how many minutes will the ratio of lengths be 1/4?

    a. 72

    b. 96

    c. 108

    d. 126

6. Find the antiderivative of the function f(x) = e⁴ˣ.

    a. $e^{4x} + C$

    b. $(1/x)\, e^{4x} + C$

    c. $4e^{4x} + C$

    d. $(1/4)\, e^{4x} + C$

7. The initial value for function f is given by f(1) = 3. The general formula of this function is f(x) = x * (f(x - 1). What is the value of f(20)?

    a. 3 * 20!

    b. 20^3

    c. 20 * 21

    d. 600

8. Which of the following functions have the largest domain?

	F(x)
I	$(x + 1) / 9x - 2)$
II	$(x + 7) / (x^2 + 5x + 6)$
III	$(x^2 - 9) / (x + 3)$
IV	$(4x + 7) / (9x^2 - 4)$

/

a. I

b. II

c. III

d. IV

9. Find the range of the function given below:

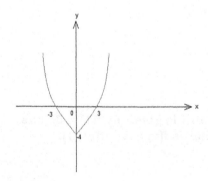

a. [-3, 3]

b. (-∞, +∞)

c. (-∞, -3) ∪ (3, +∞)

.d [-4, +∞)

10. Find the antiderivative of the function
f(x) = e^{cotx} / sin^{2}x

    a. cosx * e^{cotx} + C

    b. e^{cotx} + C

    c. -e^{cotx} + C

    d. sinx * e^{cotx} + C

Part III - Geometry

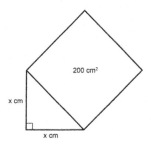

200 cm²

x cm

x cm

Note: Figure not drawn to scale

1. What is the length of the sides in the triangle above?
Assume the quadrangle in the figure above is a square.

    a. 10

    b. 20

    c. 100

    d. 40

2. Given a right triangle where a is 12 and sina=12/13, find cosa.

     a. -5/13

     b. -1/13

     c. 1/13

     d. 5/13

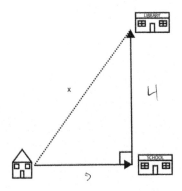

Note: Figure not drawn to scale

3. Every day starting from his home Peter travels due east 3 kilometers to the school. After school he travels due north 4 kilometers to the library. What is the distance between Peter's home and the library?

     a. 15 km

     b. 10 km

     c. 5 km

     d. 12 ½ km

4. Reflect the triangle ABC with the given mirror line m in the space below.

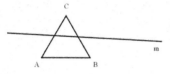

5. Reflect the rectangle ABCD with the given mirror line m in the space below.

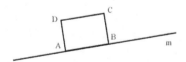

6. Reflect the quadrilateral ABCD in the coordinate plane if the mirror line is y-axis.

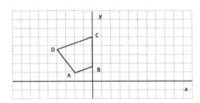

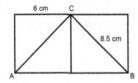

Note: figure not drawn to scale

7. Assuming the two quadrangles in the figure are identical rectangles, what is perimeter of ΔABC in the above shape?

       a. 25.5 cm

       b. 27 cm

       c. 30 cm

       d. 29 cm

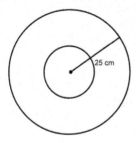

Note: figure not drawn to scale

8. What is the distance travelled by the wheel above, when it makes 175 revolutions?

    a. 87.5 п m

    b. 875 п m

    c. 8.75 п m

    d. 8750 п m

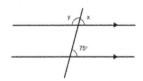

9. What is the value of the angle y?

    a. 25°

    b. 15°

    c. 30°

    d. 105°

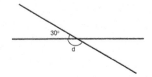

10. What is the indicated angle above?

    a. 150°

    b. 330°

    c. 60°

    d. 120°

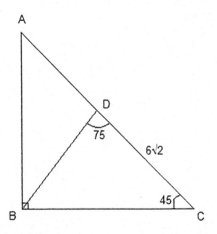

11. In the right isosceles triangles above:
|CD| = 6√2 cm, m ∠ BCD = 45°, m ∠ CDB = 75°.
Find the length of |AD|.

    a. 3√2 cm

    b. 2√6 cm

    c. 3√6 cm

    d. 6√2 cm

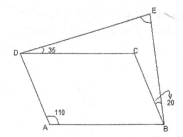

12. ABCD is a parallelogram. Find the value of m ∠ BED.

 a. 35⁰
 b. 45⁰
 c. 55⁰
 d. 65⁰

13. Find the sum of all asymptotes of the given function $(2x^2 - 5x + 4) / (x^2 - 25)$.

 a. -7
 b. -5
 c. -3
 d. 2

14. Find the constant term of the equation of the circle which has its center at (2, -5) and passes through the point (-6, 3).

 a. -99
 b. -87
 c. 87
 d. 99

15. When a triangle with corners on (3, 6), (5, 3), (3, 0) is rotated about x = 2 axis, what is the volume of the forming solid?

    a. 18π

    b. 20π

    c. 22π

    d. 24π

Part IV - Trigonometry

1. Find the domain of the function
f(x) = arccos((2x - 4) / (x - 3)).

    a. $[11/3, 5] - \{3\}$

    b. $[5/3, 3] - \{3\}$

    c. $[4, 5] - \{2\}$

    d. $[4, 15/3] - \{2\}$

2. Find the result of the expression below:
((cos4x + cos8x + cos12x) / cos4x - 1) / sin16x

    a. sin8x

    b. cos16x

    c. csc8x

    d. 2cot8x

3. Find the correct equation of the graph of the trigonometric function below.

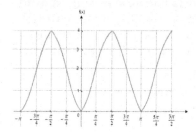

    a. 4sinx - 2

    b. 2sinx + 4

    c. 2sin2x + 2

    d. 2sin(2x - π/2) + 2

4. The relationship between the side lengths of a field is 28.|BC| = 20.|AC| = 35.|AB|. A farmer is going to plant cabbages, that is why he needs to find the area of the field, but first, he needs the measure of the corner C. What is m ∠ C rounded to the nearest degree?

    a. 25⁰

    b. 32⁰

    c. 34⁰

    d. 38⁰

5. In nuclear physics, the decay of a radioactive isotope is given by the formula A = A_0 / 2 $^{t/T1/2}$ where A_0 is the initial amount of the isotope, A is the remaining amount after decay; t is the time passing, and $T_{1/2}$ is the half-life. 2048 grams of isotope X decays for 50 days in a nuclear plant and 64 grams of it remains unweathered. Find the half-life of this isotope.

    a. 10 days

    b. 12 days

    c. 16 days

    d. 256 days

Part V - Calculus

6. Find the difference between the integral of f(x) = $2x^2$ and the area under this graph of this function using the Riemann sum with Δx = 1, within the interval [-3, 3].

    a. 12

    b. 15

    c. 18

    d. 20

7. Find the limit of the function (sin3x * ($2x^2$ + 3x - 5)) / ($6x^2$ + 15x) while x →0.

    a. -1

    b. 1

    c. 3

    d. 15

8. **Find the equation of the line tangent to the curve y = 3x³ - 8 at x = 1.**

    a. y = 9x - 14

    b. y = -9x + 14

    c. y = 9x + 16

    d. y = 18x + 16

9. **Find the local maximum of the function f(x) = x³ - 27x.**

    a. 1

    b. 3

    c. 18

    d. 27

10. **If the graph of f(x) = 3 + sin²x is rotated π/2 degrees around the x-axis, what will the volume of the forming solid be within [0, 2π]?**

    a. $7\pi^2/12$

    b. $19\pi^2/4$

    c. $9\pi^2/2$

    d. $19\pi^2$

Part VI - Statistics and Probability

1. **Find the equation of regression depending on the data below:**

Student	Math Score	History Score
A	55	85
B	45	75
C	70	35
D	90	65
E	80	80

a. ŷ = 65.8 + 0.1x

b. ŷ = 64.328 + 0.054x

c. ŷ = 64.328 + 0.54x

d. ŷ = 164.3 + 0.05x

2. There is a die and a coin. The dice is rolled and the coin is flipped the number of times given by the rolled die. If the die is rolled only once, what is the possibility to have 4 successive heads?

a. 3/64

b. 1/16

c. 3/16

d. 1/4

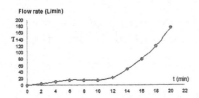

3. The scatter plot above shows the change of the water flow rate pouring from the tap by time. Which of the following statements is correct?

a. The flow is linear between [0, 4] minutes.

b. The tap is closed between [8, 10] minutes.

c. The flow increases with higher slope between [12, 20] minutes than [0, 6] minutes.

d. The flow rate linearly increases by time.

4. How many false statements are there in the below list?

- By blinding, we can avoid bias affecting the results.

- Randomization avoids bias by making each experimental unit have the same probability.

- Blinding is a method to prevent others copy our experimental results.

- For classification variables, treatments cannot be assigned randomly.

a. 1

b. 2

c. 3

d. 4

5. In a microbiology laboratory, the diameter of a sample is measured and the following values are obtained:

Number of Measurements	Measured Value (nm)
1	23
2	24.1
3	23.8
4	22.9
5	23.5
6	24
7	23.2
8	23.9
9	24.1
10	22.85

What is the mean deviation of the experiment?

    a. 0.38

    b. 0.425

    c. 0.46

    d. 0.495

6. In a certain game, players toss a coin and roll a dice. A player wins if the coin comes up heads, or the dice with a number greater than 4. In 20 games, how many times will a player win?

    a. 13

    b. 8

    c. 11

    d. 15

7. A boy has 4 red, 5 green and 2 yellow balls. He chooses two balls randomly. What is the probability that one is red and other is green?

    a. 2/11

    b. 19/22

    c. 20/121

    d. 9/11

Part VII - Mathematical Reasoning

8. Considering the statement "If a cat sees, then it has eyes", which of the following pairs have the same truth value?

    a. Inverse statement - contrapositive statement

    b. Converse statement - inverse statement

    c. Conditional statement - converse statement

    d. Contrapositive statement - conditional statement

9. Providing a direct proof, decide which of the following is the necessary and sufficient condition for $a^2 + ab$ to be odd.

a. a and b are even

b. a and b are odd

c. a is even, b is odd

d. a is odd, be is even

10. Which one of the following statements contain deductive reasoning?

A. The 6th term of the sequence 2, 4, 6, 8,... is 12.

B) Bluefish is very tasty. The fish I ate yesterday was tasty. Then, all kinds of fish are tasty.

C) All positive numbers are bigger than - 10. Therefore, 30 is bigger than - 10.

D) Hannah wore wool and she got itchy. If you wear wool, you get itchy.

11. Find the equivalent of the statement below:

$$p \rightarrow [q \rightarrow (p \cap q)]$$

a. 0

b. p'

c. q

d. 1

12. ABC that is an isosceles triangle with vertex angle A. The following are the indirect proof steps that prove that angles ABC and ACB are congruent. Which steps need to be displaced so that the steps are in order?

Statements	Reasons
I. ABC is an isosceles triangle.	Given
II. A is the vertex angle of the triangle.	Given
III. Angles ABC and ACB are not congruent.	Assumption of direct proof.
IV. Angles ABC and ACB are congruent.	The negation is false.
V. Angles ABC and ACB are congruent.	The angles opposite to the congruent legs of an isosceles triangle are congruent.
VI. Contradiction	Angles ABC and ACB cannot be both equal and unequal.
VII. Side AB is equal to AC.	Legs of an isosceles triangle are congruent.

    a. IV and VII

    b. III and VII

    c. V and VI

    d. III and VI

13. Most people in oil producing countries are rich. I live in an oil producing country. I am rich. If the first 2 statements are true, then the third statement is:

    a. True

    b. False

    c. Uncertain

14. Science can explain all events. Making a decision is an event. Science cannot explain how I make a decision. If the first 2 statements are true, then the third statement is:

    a. True

    b. False

    c. Uncertain

Skills and Competencies

Part I - Algebra

1. Rewrite expressions with radical and rational numbers

2. Perform operations with complex numbers

3. Operations on matrices

4. Solve quadratics

5. Solve quadratics

6. Factor Quadratics

7. Factor Quadratics

8. Perform operations with polynomials

9. Perform operations with polynomials

10. Graph quadratics

11. Identify graphs of linear equations or inequality with 2 variables on coordinate plane

12. Linear equations with 2 variables

13. Solve quadratic word problems

14. Linear equations with 1 variable

15. Determine slope of a line

16. Real world problems with inverse ratio

17. Simplify and approximate radicals

18. Solve equations with rational or radical expressions

19. Perform operations with rational numbers

20. Negative exponents

Part II - Functions

1. Calculate the domain of a function

2. Calculate antiderivatives

3. Calculate the Determine the first derivative of a function

4. Linear Functions

5. Perform operations with functions

6. Use antiderivatives for algebraic, trigonometric, exponential, and logarithmic functions

7. Functions - sequences and recursive functions

8. Determine the domain and range of a given table of values

9. Determine the domain and range from a given graph of a function

10. Use antiderivatives for algebraic, trigonometric, exponential, and logarithmic functions

Part III - Geometry

1. Apply the Pythagorean theorem to solve problems

2. Properties of triangles

3. Apply the Pythagorean theorem to solve problems

4. Apply properties of reflection

5. Apply properties of reflection

6. Apply properties of reflection

7. Calculate perimeter

8. Calculate perimeter

9. Solve problems using interior and exterior angles

10. Solve problems using interior and exterior angles

11. Solving problems using the properties of 30-60-90 and 45-45-90 triangles

12. Solve problems using the properties of quadrilaterals

13. Determine the asymptotes of an equation or graph

14. Determine the equation, graph, center or radius or a circle, given appropriate information

15. Rotate geometric form

Part IV - Trigonometry

1. Determine equations of graphs or circular / trigonometric functions and their inverse

2. Prove circular / trigonometric function identities or apply them to solve problems

3. Analyze graphs of trigonometric functions (amplitude, period, phase shift)

4. Solve real-world problems involving triangles using the law of sines or the law of cosines

5. Apply trigonometric functions to real world phenomena

Part V - Calculus

6. Interpret derivatives and definite integrals as limits (difference quotients, slope, Riemann sums area)

7. Determine limits using theorems concerning sums, products and quotients of functions

8. Determine the slope or equation of a tangent line at a point on a curve

9. Use the Determine the first derivative of a function in various representations to determine increasing and decreasing intervals or extrema

10. Solve distance, area, and volume problems using integration

Part VI - Statistics and Probability

1. Interpret data on two categorical and quantitative variables (e.g., regression)

2. Calculate probability with dependent and independent values

3. Analyze and interpret types of data - box plots, histograms, scatter plots

4. Identify the processes used to design and conduct statistical experiments including possible sources of bias.

5. Infer and justify conclusions from sample surveys, experimental data, and observational studies

6. Calculate probability with dependent and independent variables.

7. Calculate probability with dependent and independent variables.

Part VII - Mathematical Reasoning

8. Identify and compare the converse, inverse, and contrapositive of conditional statement

9. Analyze mathematical assertions with proofs (direct, indirect, mathematical induction, algebraic)

10. Identify examples of inductive or deductive reasoning

11. Evaluate arguments and draw conclusions based on a data
12. Analyze mathematical assertions within proofs (e.g., direct, indirect, mathematical induction, algebraic)

13. Predict logical conclusions from statements

14. Predict logical conclusions from statements

Answer Key

Part I - Algebra

1. B
In this question, notice that there are different degrees of roots. When no number is mentioned as degree, it is square root. There are also 3rd and 4th degree of roots in this question. When taking the nth root of a number, we need to consider in the opposite direction. The nth root of the number is the number of which nth power is the number inside the root. So, $\sqrt{(4/9)} = \sqrt{4}/\sqrt{9} = 2/3$ since the square of 2 is 4 and the square of 3 is 9. Similarly; $\sqrt[3]{125} = \sqrt[3]{5^3} = 5$ and $\sqrt[4]{81} = \sqrt[4]{3^4} = 3$. Inserting these equivalences and doing the fractional operations, step by step solution is as follows:

$(\sqrt{(4/9)} * 3/8) / ((\sqrt[3]{125} / \sqrt[4]{81}) / 4 - 1/12) = (2/3 * 3/8) / (5/3 * 1/4 - 1/12)$
$= (1/4) / (5/12 - 1/12)$
$= (1/4) / ((5 - 1) / 12) = (1/4) / (4/12) = 1/4 * 12/4 = 3/4$

2. B
We know that $i^2 = -1$. However, in this question, we see high powers of i. We need to use modular arithmetic techniques to solve this problem:

$i^0 = 1$
$i^1 = i$
$i^2 = -1$
$i^3 = -i$
$i^4 = 1$
$i^5 = i$

This means that every 4 powers; we obtain i. So, by dividing the powers by 4; the remainder of the division operation will lead us to the result of powers:

$18/4 \rightarrow$ remainder = 2
$5/4 \rightarrow$ remainder = 1
$162/4 \rightarrow$ remainder = 2
$39/4 \rightarrow$ remainder = 3

Then;

$(i^{18} - i^5 + 4i^{162} - i^{39}) / (i^2 - 1) = (i^2 - i + 4 * i^2 - i^3) / (-1 - 1)$
$= (-1 - i - 4 * 1 + i) / (-2)$
$= (-5) / (-2) = 5/2$

3. D
Notice that the dimensions for matrix A and B are 2 x 2 and 2 x 2, respectively. In matrix multiplication; the dimensions are important. Since A * X = B, the dimensions of matrix X should be 2 x 2. Say matrix X is as follows:

$$X = \begin{bmatrix} a & b \\ c & d \end{bmatrix} \quad \text{So,} \quad \begin{bmatrix} 1 & 4 \\ 1 & 3 \end{bmatrix} \begin{bmatrix} a & b \\ c & d \end{bmatrix} = \begin{bmatrix} 2 & 2 \\ 5 & 1 \end{bmatrix}$$

Now, write equations obtained from matrix multiplication:

1a + 4c = 2 ... (I)
1b + 4d = 2 ... (II)
1a + 3c = 5 ... (III)
1b + 3d = 1 ... (IV)

Now, we have 4 unknowns and 4 equations which means that we will be able to find the values of a, b, c and d. Using equations (I) and (III), we will find a and c; using equations (II) and (IV), we will find b and d:

$\quad$ 1a + 4c = 2 ... (I)
- / 1a + 3c = 5 ... (III)
4c - 3c = 2 - 5
c = -3

Inserting this value into equation (I): 1a + 4(- 3) = 2
a -12 = 2
a = 14
$\quad$ 1b + 4d = 2 ... (II)
- / 1b + 3d = 1 ... (IV)
4d - 3d = 2 - 1
d = 1

Inserting this value into equation (II): $1b + 4(1) = 2$
$b + 4 = 2$
$b = -2$

So, Matrix X = $\begin{bmatrix} a & b \\ c & d \end{bmatrix}$ is:

$X = \begin{bmatrix} 14 & -2 \\ -3 & 1 \end{bmatrix}$

4. A
$2x^2 - 3x = 0$ ... we see that both of the terms contain x; so we can take it out as a factor:
$x(2x - 3) = 0$ ... two terms are multiplied and the result is zero. This means that either of the terms or, both can be equal to zero:

$x = 0$ ... this is one of the solutions

$2x - 3 = 0 \rightarrow 2x = 3 \rightarrow x = 3/2 \rightarrow x = 1.5$ ... this is the second solution.

So, the solutions are 0 and 1.5.

5. A
To solve the equation, we need the equation in the form $ax^2 + bx + c = 0$.

$x^2 - 9x + 14 = 0$ is already in this form.

The quadratic formula to find the roots of a quadratic equation is:

$x_{1,2} = (-b \pm \sqrt{\Delta}) / 2a$ where $\Delta = b^2 - 4ac$ and is called the discriminant of the quadratic equation.

In our question, the equation is $x^2 - 9x + 14 = 0$. By remembering the form $ax^2 + bx + c = 0$:

$a = 1, b = -9, c = 14$

So, we can find the discriminant first, and then the roots of the equation:

$\Delta = b^2 - 4ac = (-9)^2 - 4 * 1 * 14 = 81 - 56 = 25$

$x_{1,2} = (-b \pm \sqrt{\Delta}) / 2a = (-(-9) \pm \sqrt{25}) / 2 = (9 \pm 5) / 2$

This means that the roots are,

$x_1 = (9 - 5) / 2 = 2$ and $x_2 = (9 + 5) / 2 = 7$

6. D
$9x^2 - 6x + 12 = 3 * \underline{3}x^2 - 2 * \underline{3}x + \underline{3} * 4 = 3(3x^2 - 2x + 4)$

7. A
$x^3y^3 - x^2y^8 = x * \underline{x^2y^3} - \underline{x^2y^3} * y^5 = x^2y^3(x - y^5)$

8. A
Write in standard form $(3y^5 + y^4 + 2y^3 - 2y + 5) - (2y^5 + 3y^3 + 7y + 2)$
Arrange in columns of like terms and subtract bottom row

$$3y^5 + y^4 + 2y^3 - 2y + 5$$
$$-2y^5 - 3y^3 - 7y - 2$$
$$\overline{}$$
$$y^5 + y^4 - y^3 - 9y + 3$$

9. B
$(-3x^2 + 2x + 6) + (-x^2 - x - 1)$

$= -3x^2 + 2x + 6 - x^2 - x - 1$ ... we write similar terms together:

$= -3x^2 - x^2 + 2x - x + 6 - 1$ ... we operate within the same terms:

$= -4x^2 + x + 5$

10. D
The coordinates where f "(x) is zero give the vertexes of the function. Here, we observe that the second derivative of the function is equal to zero when x is -1, 2, 4 and 7.

Then the sum of these values is: $-1 + 2 + 4 + 7 = 12$.

11. C
First we need to find the equation of the boundary line that is the dashed line. We are given that, it passes through points (5, 0) and (0, 2).

When we know two points on a line, we can find the line formula by first finding the slope (m) of the line using:

$m = (y_2 - y_1) / (x_2 - x_1)$

Here, say the 1st point is (5, 0) and the second is (0, 2):

$m = (y_2 - y_1) / (x_2 - x_1) = (2 - 0) / (0 - 5) = -2/5$

Now, since we know the value of the slope, we can write the line equation by using the formula:

$y - y_1 = m(x - x_1)$

$y - 0 = (-2/5)(x - 5)$

$y = -2x/5 + 2$

Now, notice that the boundary line is dashed; it is not continuous. This means that the inequality does not cover equality to - 2x/5 + 2. Now, we need to decide if the answer is y > (-2/5) x + 2 or y < (-2/5) x + 2. The easiest way to understand this is to insert the coordinates of the origin (0, 0) into the inequalities. Since the origin is inside the shaded region, (0, 0) should satisfy the inequality:

$0 <$ or $> - 2 * 0 / 5 + 2$

$0 <$ or > 2

$0 < 2$

Since 0 < 2 is the correct statement; the inequality representing the graph is y < (-2/5) x + 2.

12. C
First, we need to arrange the two equations to obtain the form ax + by = c. We see that there are 3 and 2 in the denominators of both equations. If we equate all at 6, then we can cancel all 6 in the denominators and have straight equations:

Equate all denominators at 6:

$2(4x + 5y)/6 = 3(x - 3y)/6 + 4 * 6/6$ ... Now we can cancel 6 in the denominators:

8x + 10y = 3x - 9y + 24 ... We can collect x and y terms on left side of the equation:

8x + 10y - 3x + 9y = 24

5x + 19y = 24 ... Equation (I)

Arrange the second equation:

3(3x + y)/6 = 2(2x + 7y)/6 - 1 * 6/6 ... Now we can cancel 6 in the denominators:

9x + 3y = 4x + 14y - 6 ... We can collect x and y terms on left side of the equation:

9x + 3y - 4x - 14y = -6

5x - 11y = -6 ... Equation (II)

Now, we have two equations and two unknowns x and y. By writing the two equations one under the other and operating, we can find one unknowns first, and find the other next:

5x + 19y = 24

-1/ 5x - 11y = -6 ... If we substitute this equation from the upper one, 5x cancels -5x:

5x + 19y = 24

-5x + 11y = 6 ... Summing side-by-side:

5x - 5x + 19y + 11y = 24 + 6

30y = 30 ... Dividing both sides by 30:

y = 1

Inserting y = 1 into either of the equations, we can find the value of x. Choosing equation I:

5x + 19 * 1 = 24

5x = 24 - 19

5x = 5 ... Dividing both sides by 5:

x = 1

So, x = 1 and y = 1 is the solution; it is shown as (1, 1).

13. D
The area of a rectangle is found by multiplying the width to the length. If we call these sides with "a" and "b"; the area is = a * b.

We are given that a * b = 20 cm² ... Equation I

One side is increased by 1 and the other by 2 cm. So new side lengths are "a + 1" and "b + 2."

The new area is (a + 1)(b + 2) = 35 cm² ... Equation II

Using equations I and II, we can find a and b:

ab = 20

(a + 1)(b + 2) = 35 ... We need to distribute the terms in parenthesis:

ab + 2a + b + 2 = 35

We can insert ab = 20 to the above equation:

20 + 2a + b + 2 = 35

2a + b = 35 - 2 - 20

2a + b = 13 ... This is one equation with two unknowns. We need to use another information to have two equations with two unknowns which leads us to the solution. We know that ab = 20. So, we can use a = 20/b:

2(20/b) + b = 13

40/b + b = 13 ... We equate all denominators to "b" and eliminate it:

40 + b² = 13b

b² - 13b + 40 = 0 ... We can use the roots by factoring. We

try to separate the middle term -13b to find common factors with b^2 and 40 separately:

b^2 - 8b - 5b + 40 = 0 ... Here, we see that b is a common factor for b^2 and -8b, and -5 is a common factor for -5b and 40:

b(b - 8) - 5(b - 8) = 0 Here, we have b times b - 8 and -5 times b - 8 summed up. This means that we have b - 5 times b - 8:

(b - 5)(b - 8) = 0

This is true when either, or both the expressions in the parenthesis are equal to zero:

b - 5 = 0 ... b = 5

b - 8 = 0 ... b = 8

So we have two values for b which means we have two values for 'a' as well. To find a, we can use any equation we have. Use a = 20/b.

If b = 5, a = 20/b → a = 4

If b = 8, a = 20/b → a = 2.5

So, (a, b) pairs for the sides of the original rectangle are: (4, 5) and (2.5, 8). These are found in (b) and (c) answer choices.

14. A
-x - 7 = -3x - 9
-x + 3x = -9 + 7
2x = -2
x = (-2):2
x = -1

15. A
If we know the coordinates of two points on a line, we can find the slope (m) with the below formula:

m = $(y_2 - y_1)/(x_2 - x_1)$ where (x_1, y_1) represent the coordinates of one point and (x_2, y_2) the other.

In this question:

(-9, 6) : x_1 = -9, y_1 = 6

(18, -18) : x_2 = 18, y_2 = -18

Inserting these values into the formula:

m = (-18 - 6)/(18 - (-9)) = (-24)/(27) ... Simplifying by 3:

m = -8/9

16. D
This is an inverse ratio problem. There are 6 workers in the beginning. Assume that each worker completes x work per day. Then, 6 workers will complete 6x work per day. On the second day, one worker leaves; so 5x work will be completed. The next day 4x and eventually 3x work will be completed on the 4th day. Since the job is completed in 4 days; 6x + 5x + 4x + 3x = 18x is the total work done. If no one leaves the work; there will be 6x work completed per day. As we know, the total work is 18x, so,

18x / 6x = 3 days, so 6 workers would complete the construction of the wall.

17. B
First, notice that the numbers within the roots are not prime numbers, so we need to search for perfect squares to take out of the root and prepare for the possibility to simplify:

(√75 - 3√48) / √147 + 20 = (√(3.25) - 3√(3.16)) / √(3.49) + √(5.4)

= (√(3.52) - 3√(3.42)) / √(3.72) + √(5.22)

= (5√3 - 12√3) / 7√3 + 2√5

= (- 7√3) / 7√3 + 2√5 = - 1 + 2√5

Now, we need to find the approximate value of √5 to tenths digit. To find the square root of 5 manually, we need to separate the number with all decimals in pairs starting from right. First, we search for the highest square smaller than 5. That is 4 and its square root is 2. In the upper part, we write this as the integer part of the square root of 5, then subtract 4 from 5. We obtain 1, then we write down double zero next to it. On the left hand side, we multiply 2 by 2 and obtain 4. Now, we search for a number to write next to 4 that will make the highest number smaller than 100 when multiplied by itself. We notice that 42 times 2 is 84 that is the highest. (43 times 3 exceeds 100) We write number "2" next to the integer part 2, after decimal point. Then, we subtract 84 from 100 and obtain 1600 by adding double zero next to the difference. On the left side; we multiply number "2" in 42 by 2 and obtain 4. Since this is smaller than 10, we directly write 4 in 42 in front of the 4 obtained by multiplication. Now, we search for a number to write next to 44 that will make the highest number smaller than 1600 when multiplied by itself. That is 3. We write this next to 2.2 and we continue so on. This operation can be continued infinitely.

```
              2.236...
2        √5.00 00 00 ....
          - 4
42        1 00
          - 84
443         16 00
          -  1329
4496          271 00
          -     26976
                 124
```

$\sqrt{5}$ = 2.236... continues. We need to round this result to tenths digit; that is 2.2.

So, the result - 1 + 2$\sqrt{5}$ is approximated to -1 + 2 * 22 = -1 + 4.4 = 3.4

18. D
In this type of question with one root within the other, we need to reduce the expression to one root with one degree that is found by multiplying all degrees of roots that follow each other.

Meanwhile; while taking a number inside a root, we need to take its power that is the degree of the root:

$$\sqrt[4]{(2 * \sqrt[3]{4})} * \sqrt[3]{\sqrt{8}} = \sqrt[6]{(4 * \sqrt[2]{2^{x+1}})}$$
$$= \sqrt[4.3]{(2^3 * 4)} * \sqrt[3.2]{8} = \sqrt[6.2]{(4^2 * 2^{x+1})}$$

Notice that every term is a power of 2, so write all of them in base 2:

$$= \sqrt[12]{(2^3 * 2^2)} * \sqrt[6]{2^3} = \sqrt[12]{(2^4 * 2^{x+1})}$$
$$= \sqrt[12]{2^5} * \sqrt[6]{2^3} = \sqrt[12]{2^{x+5}}$$
$$= 2^{5/12} * 2^{3/6} = 2^{(x+5)/12}$$
$$= 2^{(5/12 + 1/2)} = 2^{(x+5)/12}$$

Now that the bases are the same, we can equate the powers:

5/12 + 1/2 = (x + 5) / 12
(5 + 6) / 12 = (x + 5) / 12
11 = x + 5
x = 6

19. A
((1 - 1/3) * (1 + 1/5)) / (1/8 * 4/5 - 1/3)
First, we need to do the operations inside parenthesis and the multiplications. In the nominator, we need to do one subtraction and one addition operation:

= ((3/3 - 1/3) * (5/5 + 1/5)) / (4 / (8 * 5) - 1/3)

Now, we can subtract and add the fractions having the same denominators. Also, in the denominator; numbers 4 and 8 can be simplified by 4:

= (2/3 * 6/5) / (1/10 - 1/3)

Here, 3 and 6 are simplified by 3; meanwhile, the subtraction operation in the denominator is performed by the use of lcm (least common multiplier) that is 30 for 3 and 10:

= (4/5) / (3/30 - 10/30)
= (4/5) / ((3 - 10) / 30)
= (4/5) / (-7/30)

Now, we have two fractions that are divided. We can turn this operation into multiplication by simply changing the values of the denominator and the numerator of the second fraction as below:

= (4/5) * (-30/7)

Note that we use parenthesis since the second fraction is negative. We can also write the minus sign in the front of the expression. Now, we can simplify 30 and 5 by 5:

= -(4 * 6) / 7 = -24/7

20. C

Our aim is to write the expression leaving no letter containing term in the denominator. Remember that, if a term is taken from the denominator to numerator or vice versa; its power changes sign. We can do power operations provided that the bases are the same:

$(a^3(4a)^{-2}b^8c) / (a^6(2a)^{-3}b^5c^{12}) = (a^34^{-2}a^{-2}b^8c) / (a^62^{-3}a^{-3}b^5c^{12})$

$= (a^{(3-2)}(1/16) b^8c) / (a^{(6-3)}(1/8) b^5c^{12}) = ((1/16)ab^8c) / ((1/8) a^3b^5c^{12})$

$= (1/16) (8/1) (a^{(1-3)}b^{(8-5)}c^{(1-12)}$

$= (1/2)a^{-2}b^3c^{-11}$

Part II - Functions

1. C

If the function is $f(x) = x$; this will be definable for every x. However, there are some cases where we need to eliminate some ranges of x. In this question, there is a square root operation and a denominator.

The expression inside the square root cannot be negative. So:

$x + 7 \geq 0$

$x \geq -7$

On the other hand; the denominator cannot be zero since number divided by zero is not definable:

$x - 3 \neq 0$

$x \neq 3$

We have two limitations; x can neither be smaller than -7

nor equal to 3. So, the domain for this function is:

[-7, +∞) - {3} or we can also show by: [-7, 3) ∪ (3, +∞).

2. D
There are two ways to check the statements: We can take the derivative of the antiderivatives to find out if we obtain the functions given or not. Else, we can integrate the given functions to check if we obtain the given antiderivatives or not. Choose the second option:

1. f(x) = x sin3x

We will perform ∫x sin3x dx. Here, we need to apply the rule: ∫udv = uv - ∫vdu:

u = x → by integration: du = dx

dv = sin3x dx → by integration: v = (-1/3) cos3x

∫x sin3x dx = x (- 1/3) cos3x - ∫(-1/3) cos3x dx

= (-1/3) x cos3x + (1/9) sin3x + C

= (-1/3) [x cos3x - (1/3) sin3x] + C

There is a minus mistake in the answer given in the question, so the antiderivative given for 1 is wrong.

2. f(x) = 1 / (2√(3x³))

We will perform ∫dx / (2√(3x³)). After some organization:

∫dx / (2√(3x³)) = (1 / 2√3) ∫x $^{-3/2}$ dx = ((1 / 2√3) * (x $^{-3/2+1}$) / (-3/2 + 1)) + C

= ((1 / 2√3) * (x $^{-1/2}$) / (-1/2)) + C

= -1 / √(3x) + C

This is the same result with the antiderivative given in the question; that is correct.

3. D
First, write the general formulas for the terms of each se-

quence.

Sequence a_n starts with 2 and following terms are always 2 plus the previous. Then, we conclude that:

$a_{k+1} = 2 + 2k$

Similarly, sequence b_n starts with 4 and following terms are always 5 plus the previous. Then, we can write:

$b_{m+1} = 4 + 5m$

We are searching for the cases when $2 + 2k = 4 + 5m$:

$2 + 2k = 4 + 5m$

$2k = 4 + 5m - 2$

$2k = 5m + 2$

$k = 5m/2 + 1$

Now, the question is: How many integer m values are there that result in integer k values in this equation?

We know that there are 50 terms in each sequence. So, the maximum value for both $k + 1$ and $m + 1$ is 50. Notice that m is divided by 2. Since the addition part 1 is an integer itself, we need to focus on the term $5m/2$. m values should be even numbers; say $m = 2a$, a is an integer. Also, we have the limitation that k can be 49 the most:

$49 \geq (5 * 2a. / 2 + 1$

$48 \geq 5a$

$48/5 \geq a$

$9.6 \geq a$

So, a is maximum 9. This means that 10 integers can be assigned to a which are integers from 0 to 9. So, 10 integers can be assigned to m that are 2 times integers from 0 to 9 (0, 2, 4, ... , 18). As a result; there are 10 possible cases when $2 + 2k = 4 + 5m$, meaning that there are 10 terms common in sequences $\{a_n\}$ and $\{b_n\}$.

4. A
To derive a function which is a fraction and both numerator and denominator depend on x, we use the following general formula:

$f(x) = g(x) / h(x) \rightarrow f'(x) = df/dx = (dg/dx * h - dh/dx * g) / h^2$

So,

$(d/dx)((x^3 + 1)/(x - 2)) = [((d/dx)(x^3 + 1)) * (x - 2) - ((d/dx)(x - 2)) * (x^3 + 1)] / (x - 2)^2$

$= (3x^2(x - 2) - 1(x^3 + 1)) / (x - 2)^2$

$= (3x^3 - 6x^2 - x^3 - 1) / (x^2 - 4x + 4)$

$= (2x^3 - 6x^2 - 1) / (x^2 - 4x + 4)$

We are asked to do the polynomial division operation above and find the remainder:

```
  2x³ - 6x² - 1   |  x² - 4x + 4
- / 2x³ - 8x² + 8x      2x + 2
    2x² - 8x - 1
- / 2x² - 8x + 8
```

          -9 is the remainder

5. C
Two candles have the same length differing in burning speeds. Since they burn in 2 and 3 hours, considering their lcm (least common multiple), say that their lengths are 6x.

First candle burns 3x in an hour. After t hours, 6x - 3x.t is left. This candle burns faster than the other.

Second candle burns 2x in an hour. After t hours, 6x - 2x.t is left.

Setting the related equation:

$(6x - 3xt) / (6x - 2xt) = 1/4$

4(6x - 3xt) = 6x - 2xt

24x - 12xt = 6x - 2xt

18x = 10xt

t = 18/10 = 1.8 hours

1.8 hours = 1.8 * 60 = 108 minutes

6. D
The antiderivative of a function f is the function that when it is derived, f is obtained. The antiderivative of e4x is:

$\int e^{4x}\, dx = (1/4)\ e^{4x} + C$

7. A
Let us start by writing some values of the function:
x = 1 : f(1) = 3

x = 2 : f(2) = 2 * f(1)

x = 3 : f(3) = 3 * f(2) = 3 * 2 * f(1)

x = 4 : f(4) = 4 * f(3) = 4 * 3 * 2 * f(1)

x = 5 : f(5) = 5 * f(4) = 5 * 4 * 3 * 2 * f(1)

Notice that the expansion of f(n) contains n! times f(1). So,

f(n) = n! * f(1)

f(n) = 3 * n!

is the general formula of the function. Then,

f(20) = 3 * 20!

8. C
Without any restrictions, the domain of a function is (-∞, +∞). The restrictions are found by checking the denominator of the function. If there are any values that make the denominator zero; since division by zero is undefined, these x values should be eliminated from the domain:

f(x) = (x + 1) / (x - 2) : Notice that the denominator is x - 2 and x = 2 value makes it zero, so makes the function is undefined. The domain of this function is $(-\infty, +\infty) - \{2\}$.

$f(x) = (x + 7) / (x^2 + 5x + 6)$: Notice that the denominator is $x^2 + 5x + 6$ which can be factored as $(x + 2)(x + 3)$.

Then, $x = -2$ and $x = -3$ values make the denominator zero, so the function is undefined. The domain of this function is $(-\infty, +\infty) - \{-3, -2\}$.

$f(x) = (x^2 - 9) / (x + 3)$: Notice that first, it is possible to simplify the function:

$f(x) = (x^2 - 9) / (x + 3) = (x + 3)(x - 3) / (x + 3) = x - 3$. Then, the denominator has vanished; the domain of this function is $(-\infty, +\infty)$.

$f(x) = (4x + 7) / (9x^2 - 4)$: Notice that the denominator is $9x^2 - 4$ which can be factored as $(3x - 2)(3x + 2)$. It is not possible to simplify.

Then, $x = 2/3$ and $x = -2/3$ values make the denominator zero, so make the function undefined. The domain of this function is $(-\infty, +\infty) - \{-2/3, 2/3\}$.

Function $(x^2 - 9) / (x + 3)$ has the largest domain.

9. D
The range of a graph is the set of y values of the function. Examining the graph above, we see that for all x values, y values are equal and above -4. In other words; y cannot have values smaller than -4. So, the range is $[-4, +\infty)$.

10. C
The antiderivative of a function f is the function that when it is derived, f is obtained. The antiderivative of $e^{\cot x} / \sin^2 x$ is: $\int (e^{\cot x} / \sin^2 x)\, dx$

Here, we need to perform change of variables to be able to connect cotx to $\sin^2 x$. Let us say:

$\cot x = u$ ... Deriving this expression:

$-\csc^2 x\, dx = du \rightarrow (-1/\sin^2 x)\, dx = du$

$\int (e^{\cot x} / \sin^2 x)\, dx = \int -e^u\, du = -e^u + C = -e^{\cot x} + C$

Part III - Geometry

1. A
If we call one side of the square "a," the area of the square will be a^2.

We know that $a^2 = 200$ cm^2.

On the other hand; there is an isosceles right triangle. Using the Pythagorean Theorem:

(Hypotenuse)^2 = (Adjacent Side)^2 + (Opposite Side)^2 Where the hypotenuse is equal to one side of the square. So,

$a^2 = x^2 + x^2$

$200 = 2x^2$

$200/2 = 2x^2/2$

$100 = x^2$

$x = \sqrt{100}$

$x = 10$ cm

2. D
To understand this question better, let us draw a right triangle by writing the given data on it:

Note: Figure not drawn to scale

The side opposite angle a is named by a.

sin a = length of the opposite side / length of the hypotenuse = 12/13 is given.

cos a = length of the adjacent side / length of the hypotenuse = b/13

We use the Pythagorean Theorem to find the value of b:

(Hypotenuse)^2 = (Opposite Side)^2 + (Adjacent Side)^2

$c^2 = a^2 + b^2$

$13^2 = 12^2 + b^2$

$169 = 144 + b^2$

$b^2 = 169 - 144$

$b^2 = 25$

$b = 5$

So,

$\cos a = b/13 = 5/13$

3. C
We see that two legs of a right triangle form by Peter's movements and we are asked to find the length of the hypotenuse. We use the Pythagorean Theorem:

$(\text{Hypotenuse})^2 = (\text{Adjacent side})^2 + (\text{Opposite side})^2$

$h^2 = a^2 + b^2$

We know that a and b are 3 km and 4 km. So,

$h^2 = 3^2 + 4^2$

$h^2 = 9 + 16$

$h^2 = 25$

$h = \sqrt{25}$

$h = 5 \text{ km}$

4.
We reflect points A, B and C against the mirror line m at the right angle and we connect the new points A', B' and C'. The process is the same even though the points of the triangle are not on the same side of the mirror line.

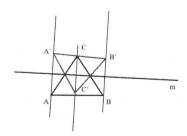

5.

We reflect points C and D against the mirror line m at the right angle. Since points A and B are already on the mirror line, we can't reflect them and that's why A coincides with point A' , and the same goes for points B and B'.

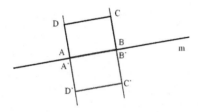

6.

The Apply properties of reflection process is the same in the coordinate plane. Here, our mirror line is y-axis, so we reflect points A and D, and points B and C are already on the mirror line, so we don't reflect them.

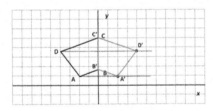

7. D

Perimeter of a triangle = sum of all three sides.
Here, Perimeter of ΔABC = |AC| + |CB| + |AB|.

Since the triangle is located in the middle of two adjacent and identical rectangles, we find the side lengths using these rectangles:

|AB| = 6 + 6 = 12 cm

|CB| = 8.5 cm

|AC| = |CB| = 8.5 cm

Perimeter = |AC| + |CB| + |AB| = 8.5 + 8.5 + 12 = 29 cm

8. A

The wheel travels $2\pi r$ distance when it makes one revolution. Here, r stands for radius. The radius is given as 25 cm in the figure. So,

$2\pi r = 2\pi * 25 = 50\pi$ cm is the distance travelled in one revolution.

In 175 revolutions: $175 * 50\pi = 8750\pi$ cm is travelled.

We are asked to find the distance in meters.

1 m = 100 cm So,

8750π cm = $8750\pi / 100 = 87.5\pi m$

9. D

Two parallel lines intersected by a third line with angles of 75°
x = 75° (corresponding angles)
x + y = 180°(supplementary angles)
y = 180° - 75°
y = 105°

10. A

The angles opposite both angles 30° & angle d are respectively equal to vertical angles.
2(30°+ d) = 360°
2d = 360° - 60°
2d = 300°
d = 150°

11. B

Drawing a height dividing 75⁰; we obtain a small triangle EDC that is similar to the large triangle BAC.

In a 45 - 45 - 90 triangle; the legs are $1/\sqrt{2}$ of the hypotenuse. So; |DE| = |EC| = 6 cm:

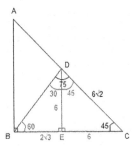

Then, in triangle BED; |BE| that is the opposite side of 300, is 1/√3 of |ED| that is opposite to 600.

So,

|BE| = 2√3 cm.

ΔBAC ~ ΔEDC

Meaning that |EC| / |BE| = |DC| / |AD|

6 / 2√3 = 6√2 / |AD| → |AD| = 2√6 cm

12. C
In a parallelogram, opposite located angles have the same value.

So, m ∠ BCD = m ∠ DAB = 110⁰

m ∠ BCD = m ∠ EDC + m ∠ CBE + m ∠ BED is a shortcut geometric property for practical use:

110 = 35 + 20 + m ∠ BED

m ∠ BED = 110 - 55 = 55⁰

13. D
The vertical asymptote is found by searching the values that make the function undefined. If there is any value to make the denominator zero, then it is the vertical asymptote:

$x^2 - 25 = 0$

x = 5 and x = -5

So; x = -5 and x = 5 are the vertical asymptotes.

Notice that numerator and denominator are of the same degree (2). So, there is a non-zero horizontal asymptote and there is no slant asymptote. Dividing the leading terms; we obtain the horizontal asymptote:

$2x^2 / x^2 = 2$

The sum of all asymptotes belonging to this function is -5 + 5 + 2 = 2.

14. A
Applying the general form $(x - a)^2 + (y - b)^2 = r^2$, we have:

$(x - 2)^2 + (y + 5)^2 = r^2$

If the circle passes through the point (-6, 3); the radius is the line connecting the center (2, -5) and (-6, 3):

$r^2 = (2 - (-6))^2 + (-5 - 3)^2$

$= 8^2 + 8^2$

$= 128$

Then;

$(x - 2)^2 + (y + 5)^2 = 128$

Let us expand the equation to find the constant term:

$(x - 2)^2 + (y + 5)^2 = 128$

$x^2 - 4x + 4 + y2 + 10y + 25 = 128$

$x^2 - 4x + y^2 + 10y - 99 = 0$

The constant term of the equation is -99.

15. B
This question can be solved by just using imagination. However, let us use the coordinate system for a better

understanding:

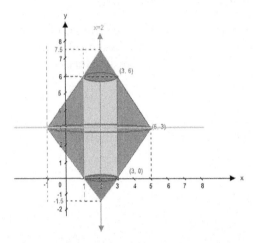

First, draw the triangle with corners (3, 0), (5, 3), (3, 6).
Then, draw the rotation axis x = 2. Then, imagine that the
triangle will rotate about axis x = 2. Notice that each corner
of the triangle is reflected across axis x = 2 to shape the
other part of the solid. The forming shape after rotation is
like two cones stuck together on their bases; endpoints cut,
and a cylinder carved from inside.

Find the volume of the cones first, then subtract the
endpoints and the cylinder inside. Do the operations as if
the outer side triangle, then we can multiply the result by 2
to find the overall volume:

We need to find the upper endpoint of the cone. With a
simple ratio within triangles, we can find it:

(3 - 2) / (5 - 2) = x / (x + (6 - 3))

1 / 3 = x / (x + 3) → 3x = x + 3 → x = 3/2 = 1.5

x is the distance between the upper endpoint of the cone and
the upper surface of the solid shape forming.
6 + 1.5 = 7.5 is the ordinate of the upper endpoint of the
cone and the height of the cut endpoint of the cone is 1.5
units. Its radius is (3 - 2) = 1 unit. Then, the volume of the
cut part is:

(Each of the end-cone volumes on the figure):
V = (πr²h) / 3

= (π * 1² * 1.5) / 3 = 0.5π

Let us calculate the volume of the cylinder that is carved out of the solid. Notice that, below the bisecting line; the height of the cylinder is (6 - 3) = 3 units and the radius is (3 - 2) = 1 unit:

(Each of the cylindrical volumes in the figure):
V = r²h = π * 1² * 3 = 3π

Now, let us calculate the volume of one cone below the bisecting line. Note that the height of one cone is (7.5 - 3) = 4.5 units and the radius is (5 - 2) = 3 units:

V = (πr²h) / 3 = (π * 3² * 4.5) / 3 = 13.5π

Now, let us find the net volume of one half of the solid shape forming after rotation:

V$_{total}$ / 2 = 13.5π - 0.5π - 3π = 10π

→V$_{total}$ = 2 * 10π = 20π

Part IV - Trigonometry

1. A
It is important to find the limitation of the arccos function.
cosx = u

arccos(cosx) = arccosu → x = arccosu

The cosine of any angle should be within the interval [-1, 1] which means that u should be within this interval:

-1 ≤ ((2x - 4) / (x - 3)) ≤ 1

-1 ≤ ((2(x - 3) + 2) / (x - 3)) ≤ 1

-1 ≤ (2 + 2 / (x - 3)) ≤ 1

-1 - 2 ≤ (2 / (x - 3)) ≤ 1 - 2

$-3 \le (2 / (x - 3)) \le -1$

$-3/2 \le (1 / (x - 3)) \le -1/2$

$2/3 \le x - 3 \le 2$

$2/3 + 3 \le x - 3 + 3 \le 2 + 3$

$11/3 \le x \le 5$

When writing $-1 \le ((2x - 4) / (x - 3)) \le 1$, notice that the denominator of the fraction is x - 3 which means that x cannot be equal to 3 since this causes an indefinite situation. So; the domain of the function is:

[11/3, 5] - {3}

2. C
Notice that there are trigonometric functions of factors of x. 4x is exactly in the middle of 3x and 5x, which means that we can use conversion formula,
cosa + cosb = 2 * cos((a + b) / 2) * cos((a - b) / 2)

Then:

cos4x + cos12x = 2 * cos((4x + 12x) / 2) * cos((4x - 12x) / 2)

= 2 * cos8x * cos(-4x)

= 2 * cos8x * cos4x

So,

((cos4x + cos8x + cos12x) / cos4x - 1) / sin16x = ((2 * cos8x * cos4x + cos4x) / cos4x - 1) / sin16x

= (cos4x (2cos8x + 1) / cos4x - 1) / sin16x

= (2cos8x + 1 - 1) / sin16x

= 2cos8x / sin16x

Using double angle formula for sine:

2cos8x / sin16x = 2cos8x / (2 * sin8x * cos8x) = 1 / sin8x = csc8x

3. D

The graph passes through the origin which means that this is a sine graph. The basic function can be taken as sinx.

The general formula of sine function is a * sin(bx - c) + d, where amplitude is found by |a|, period by $2\pi/|b|$, phase shift by c/b and vertical shift by d. Now let us find these values from the graph:

Notice that the graph oscillates between 0 and 4. This means that the amplitude is 2.

Period is the duration between two cases when the movement is in the same direction passing through the same point. Here, we see that, the period is π. Then,

$2\pi/|b| = \pi \rightarrow b = 2$

Compared to sine, this function is narrowed by factor 2 (that is b), extended by factor 2 (that is a), shifted 2 units upwards, and lastly shifted $\pi/4$ to right (that is c/b). So, c = $\pi/4$ * 2 = $\pi/2$.

Inserting the values found into the general form:

a * sin(bx - c) + d = 2sin(2x - $\pi/2$) + 2

4. C

In geometry, the side |BC| is named by a, |AC| by b, and |AB| by c:

28 *|BC| = 20 * |AC| = 35 *|AB|

28 * a = 20 * b = 35 * c

The lcm of 28, 20 and 35 is 140. So, we can say that:

a = 5k

b = 7k

c = 4k

Applying the law of cosine, we can find cosC:

$c^2 = a^2 + b^2 - 2ab\cos C$

$(4k)^2 = (5k)^2 + (7k)^2 - 2 * 5k * 7k * \cos C$

$16k^2 = 25k^2 + 49k^2 - 70k^2 * \cos C$

$70k^2 * \cos C = 58k^2$

$\cos C = 56/70$

$c = \arccos 56/70$

$C = 34.048^0$

$C = 34^0$ when rounded

$C = 34^0$ when rounded to the nearest integer.

5. A
First insert the known values into the formula given:

$A = A_0 / 2^{t/T1/2}$

$64 = 2048 / 2^{50/T1/2}$

$2^{50/T1/2} = 2048 / 64$

$2^{50/T1/2} = 32$

$2^{50/T1/2} = 2^5$

$50 / T_{1/2} = 5$

$T_{1/2} = 10$

So, the half-life of the radioactive isotope is 10 days.

Part V - Calculus

6. D

First, find the integral of the function within the interval given:

$$\int_{-3}^{3} 2x^2dx = 2(x^3 / 3) \Big|_{-3}^{3} = (2/3)(27 - (-27)) = 36$$

Now, let us draw the rectangles to be used in Riemann sum. The formula for this method is: $\sum_{i=0}^{n-1} f(x_i)\Delta x$.

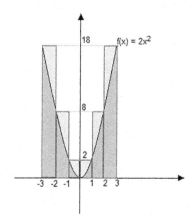

The smaller Δx value we use, the cleaner the calculation will be and the result will be closer to the integration result. In Riemann sum here, it is practical to find the total area between [0, 3] and multiply it by 2:

$$\sum_{i=0}^{n-1} f(x_i)\Delta x = 2[(1 - 0)^* 2(1)^2 + (2 - 1)^* 2(2)^2 + (3 - 2)^* 2(3)^2]$$

$$= 2[1 * 2 + 1 * 8 + 1 * 18] = 2 * 28 = 56$$

The difference of Riemann sum - integration is: 56 - 36 = 20

7. C

First, let us insert $x = 0$ into the function:

$$\lim_{x \to 0} (\sin3x * (2x^2 + 3x - 5)) / (6x^2 + 15x)$$

$$= (\sin(3*0) * (2*0^2 + 3*0 - 5)) / (6*0^2 + 15*0) = 0/0$$

The result is indefinite. Since the expression in the question is not the simplified form, let us try to simplify the function first:

$(\sin3x * (2x^2 + 3x - 5)) / (6x^2 + 15x) = (\sin3x * (2x + 5)(x - 1)) / (3x(2x + 5)) = (\sin3x * (x - 1)) / 3x$

We cannot further simplify. Now, let us try to insert $x = 0$ again:

$$\lim_{x \to 0} ((\sin3x * (x - 1)) / 3x) = 0/0$$

Remember that $\lim_{x \to 0} (\sin x / x) = 1$. Using this property:

$$\lim_{x \to 0} ((\sin3x \cdot (x - 1)) / 3x) = 1 * \lim_{x \to 0} (x - 1) = 1 * (-1) = -1$$

8. A

The first order derivative of a function is equal to the slope of the tangent line. We are asked to find the equation of the formula. Let us start with finding the slope first:
$y = 3x^3 - 8$

$y' = 9x^2$

at $x = 1$:

$y' = 9 * 1^2 = 9$ ... This is the slope.

We know that the general formula of a linear function is:
$y = mx + b$.

We know that $m = 9$. We need to determine b.

Note that at $x = 1$, $y = 3 * 1^3 - 8 = -5$. This means that at

(1, -5), the line is tangent to the curve. So, this point is on the tangent line. Inserting the coordinates will give b:

-5 = 9 * 1 + b

b = -14

So the equation of the tangent line is: y = 9x - 14.

9. B

The values that cause the first derivative of the function to be zero or indefinite are the critical points. The local minimum and maximum values are at the critical points. However, not all the critical points are extremas.

Start by taking the first derivative:

$f(x) = x^3 - 27x$

$f' = 3x^2 - 27$

Notice that no x value makes f ' indefinite. So, next find the values that satisfy f ' = 0:

$f' = 3x^2 - 27 = 0$

$3x^2 = 27$

$x^2 = 9$

x = -3 and x = 3

So, -3 and 3 are the critical points. Now, we can get through 1st derivative test. Let us mark the critical points on a number line:

There are three regions here; (-∞, -3), (-3, 3) and (3, +∞). Next, select an integer from each interval and insert into the f ' equation to see whether it is negative of positive:

(-∞, -3): x = - 1: f ' = 3(-1)² - 27 = -24: negative

(-3, 3): x = 0: f ' = 3(0)² - 27 = -27: negative

(3, +∞): x = 4: f ' = 3(4)² - 27 = 21: positive

Now, insert the signs in the number line below:

This is the sign graph for the function. Notice that before and after -3; the graph is decreasing; there is no sign switch. So, there is no minimum or maximum at this point. However, the function decreases before 3, but increases after 3. This means that there is a local maximum at x = 3.

10. B

$$V_{\text{Rotated Area}} = \pi \int_0^{2\pi} (f(x))^2 dx$$

$$= \pi \int_0^{2\pi} (3 + \sin2x)^2 dx$$

$$= \pi \int_0^{2\pi} (9 + 6\sin2x + \sin^2 2x) dx$$

$$= 9\pi \int_0^{2\pi} dx + 6\pi \int_0^{2\pi} \sin2x dx + \pi \int_0^{2\pi} \sin^2 2x dx$$

$$= 9\pi {}^*x \Big|_0^{2\pi} + 6\pi((-1/2)\cos2x) \Big|_0^{2\pi} + \pi(x/2 - \sin4x / 8) \Big|_0^{2\pi}$$

$$= 9\pi(2\pi - 0) - 3\pi(\cos4\pi - \cos0) + \pi((2\pi - 0)/2 - (\sin8\pi - \sin0)/8)$$

$$= 18\pi^2 - 0 + \pi(\pi - 0)$$

$$= 19\pi^2$$

This is the volume of the solid when rotated 2π degrees. If the graph is rotated π/2 degrees, it will scan a quarter of the total volume. That is:

19π²/4

Part VI - Statistics and Probability

1. B

The equation of regression can be shown by $\hat{y} = b_0 + b_1 x$
where coefficients b_0 and b_1 are obtained from:
$b_0 = \bar{y} - b_1 * \bar{x}$

$$b_1 = \left(\sum_{i=1}^{n} ((x_i - \bar{x})(y_i - \bar{y})) \right) / \sum_{i=1}^{n} (x_i - \bar{x})^2$$

where $\bar{x}$ and $\bar{y}$ are the mean values of math scores and history scores.

$\bar{x} = (55 + 45 + 70 + 90 + 80) / 5 = 68$

$\bar{y} = (85 + 75 + 35 + 65 + 80) / 5 = 68$

$$\sum_{i=1}^{n} (x_i - \bar{x})^2 =$$

$(55 - 68)^2 + (45 - 68)^2 + (70 - 68)^2 + (90 - 68)^2 + (80 - 68)^2 = 1330$

$$\sum_{i=1}^{n} ((x_i - \bar{x})(y_i - \bar{y}))$$

$= (55 - 68)(85 - 68) + (45 - 68)(75 - 68) + (70 - 68)(35 - 68) + (90 - 68)(65 - 68) + (80 - 68)(80 - 68) = -370$

$b_1 = -370 / 1330 = -0.2782$

$b_0 = 68 - (-0.2782) * 68 = 86.92$

Then, the equation of regression is:

$\hat{y} = -0.02782x + 86.92$

2. A

If the die is rolled for once, it can be 4, 5 or 6 since we are searching for 4 successive heads. We need to think each case separately. There are two possibilities for a coin; heads

(H) or tails (T), each possibility of $1/2$; we are searching for H. The possibility for a number to appear on the top of the die is $1/6$. Die and coin cases are disjoint events. Also, each flip of coin is independent from the other:

die: 4

coin: HHHH : 1 permutation

$P = (1/6) * (1/2) * (1/2) * (1/2) * (1/2) = (1/6) * (1/16)$

die: 5

coin: HHHHT, THHHH, HHHHH : 3 permutations

$P = (1/6) * 3 * (1/2) * (1/2) * (1/2) * (1/2) * (1/2) = (1/6) * (3/32)$

die: 6

coin: HHHHTT, TTHHHH, THHHHT, HHHHHT, THHHHH, HTHHHH, HHHHTH, HHHHHH : 8 permutations

$P = (1/6) * 8 * (1/2) * (1/2) * (1/2) * (1/2) * (1/2) * (1/2) = (1/6) * (8/64)$

The overall probability is:

$P_{all} = (1/6) * (1/16) + (1/6) * (3/32) + (1/6) * (8/64) = (1/6) * (1/16 + 3/32 + 8/64)$

$= (1/6) * (4 + 6 + 8) / 64 = (1/6) * (18/64) = 3/64$

3. C
Examining the plot; here is the information we get:

The flow rate increases linearly by time up to 6 minutes. Between 8 - 10 minutes, the flow rate is definitely constant around 20 L/min. After 12th minute; the flow starts increasing with a larger slope than it increases between 0 - 6 minutes. If the tap was closed at any time, we would observe a straight line on the horizontal axis.

4. C
The correct statements are:

- By blinding, we can avoid bias affecting the results.
- Randomisation avoids bias by making each experimental unit have the same probability.
- For classification variables, treatments cannot be assigned randomly.

The false statement is:

- Blinding is a method to prevent others copy our experimental results.

5. D
First, find the mean value of the experiment:

$\bar{x}$ = (23 + 24.1 + 23.8 + 22.9 + 23.5 + 24 + 23.2 + 23.9 + 24.1 + 22.85) / 10 = 23.535

The mean deviation is found by the formula:

$$\sigma = \sum_{i=1}^{n} |x_i - \bar{x}| / n$$

where n is the number of experiments that is 10 in this question:

σ = (|23 - 23.535| + |24.1 - 23.535| + |23.8 - 23.535| + |22.9 - 23.535| + |23.5 - 23.535| + |24 - 23.535| + |23.2 - 23.535| + |23.9 - 23.535| + |24.1 - 23.535| + |22.85 - 23.535|) / 10

= (0.535 + 0.565 + 0.265 + 0.635 + 0.535 + 0.465 + 0.335 + 0.365 + 0.565 + 0.685) / 10

= 0.495

6. A
The sample space of this event will be S = { (H,1),(H,2),(H,3),(H,4),(H,5),(H,6) (T,1),(T,2),(T,3),(T,4),(T,5),(T,6) } So there are a total of 12 outcomes and 8 winning outcomes. The probability of a win in a single event is P (W) =8/12=2/3. In

20 games the probability will be (20/3)* 2 = 13.333 or about 13.

7. A
The probability that the 1st ball drawn is red = 4/11. The probability that the 2nd ball drawn is green = 5/10. The combined probability will then be 4/11 X 5/10 = 20/110 = 2/11.

Part VII - Mathematical Reasoning

8. B
The conditional statement is given as "If a cat sees, then it has eyes." Here, we need to identify the hypothesis and the conclusion. The hypothesis (p) is "a cat sees" and the conclusion is (q) "it has eyes." We say that p → q. Let us write all versions of statement first and then analyze to find their truth values:
Converse statement: q → p: If a cat has eyes, then it sees.

This is not correct; it can have eyes as organs, but it may be blind, therefore it cannot see.

Inverse statement: ~p → ~q: If a cat does not see, then it does not have eyes.

This is not correct; seeing function may not be performed despite the presence of eyes; the cat can be blind, so we cannot 100% say that if it does not see, it does not have eyes; it can have eyes but it can be blind.

Contrapositive statement: ~q → ~p: If a cat does not have eyes, it does not see.

This is correct; if there is no eye, there is no possibility for a cat to see; eyes are the organs that function for seeing.

So; the converse and inverse statements are not true; the conditional and contrapositive statement are true. In the answer choices, we see converse - inverse statements but not conditional - contrapositive statement.

9. D

Rewriting the expression, we have: $a^2 + ab = a(a + b)$.

A. If a and b are even, let us say $a = 2k$ and $b = 2m$:

$a(a + b) = 2k(2k + 2m) = 4k(k + m)$ ... Independent of the value of $k(k + m)$; since there is an even cofactor (4), $a^2 + ab$ is even.

B) If a and b are odd, let us say $a = 2k - 1$ and $b = 2m - 1$:

$a(a + b) = (2k - 1)(2k - 1 + 2m - 1) = (2k - 1)(2k + 2m - 2) = 2(2k - 1)(k + m - 1)$ ... Independent of the value of $(2k - 1)(k + m - 1)$; since there is an even cofactor (2), $a^2 + ab$ is even.

C) If a is even, b is odd, let us say $a = 2k$ and $b = 2m - 1$:

$a(a + b) = (2k)(2k + 2m - 1) = 2(k)(2k + 2m - 1)$ ... Independent of the value of $(k)(2k + 2m - 1)$; since there is an even cofactor (2), $a^2 + ab$ is even.

D) If a is odd, b is even, let us say $a = 2k - 1$ and $b = 2m$:

$a(a + b) = (2k - 1)(2k - 1 + 2m) = (2k - 1)(2k + 2m - 1) = (2k - 1)(2(k + m) - 1)$

Let us say $k + m = n$:

$(2k - 1)(2(k + m) - 1) = (2k - 1)(2n - 1) = 4kn - 2k - 2n + 1$

Notice that 4kn is even since there is an even cofactor (4), 2k and 2n are even since there is an even cofactor (2), and 1 is an odd number. even → even → even → odd gives an odd number. Therefore, $a^2 + ab$ is odd.

10. C

To solve this problem, we need to know what deductive reasoning is. Using deductive reasoning; we obtain specific cases from generalities. On the contrary; we obtain generalities from specific cases using inductive reasoning. Let us comment on each choice given:

> **a.** We notice that every term in the sequence is 2 more than the previous. So, the 6th term will be 4 more than 8 that is 12. Here; observing the sequence, it is discovered that there is 2 difference between consecutive

terms and the rule is found. This is inductive reasoning; generality derived from specific case.

b. There are two cases observed: bluefish is tasty and the fish I ate yesterday is tasty. These are specific cases. Saying that all kinds of fish are tasty is a generality; that is inductive reasoning.

c. "All positive numbers are bigger than - 10" is a general information. Saying that 30 is bigger than - 10 is a special case deducted from the generality.

d. This is a special case that Sara wore wool and got itchy. Then, by generalizing this information - by inductive reasoning - it is claimed that "if you wear wool, you get itchy."

11. D
We need to eliminate "if" by turning it into "or":

$p \rightarrow [q \rightarrow (p \cap q)]$

$p \rightarrow [q' \cup (p \cap q)]$ ... by distribution property:

$p \rightarrow [q' \cup p) \cup \underline{(q' \cap q)}]$
$\qquad\qquad\qquad 1$

$p \rightarrow (q' \cup p)$

$p' \cup (q' \cup p)$ ... by distribution and association property:

$\underline{(p' \cup p)} \cup q'$
$\quad 1$

$1 \cup q' = 1$

12. A
In an indirect proof, first the given statements should be listed with reasons, then the assumption that is the negative of the statement to be proven should be written. Afterwards; results of the given information are listed. Then, if there is, the contradiction is mentioned. Lastly, the resulting fact is written and it is mentioned if the negation is false or not.

In this question, steps IV and VII should be displaced. Step IV should come after listing the facts which are the results of the given information; one of them is step VII.

13. C
Uncertain. I may be rich or I may not be.

14. B
False. If Science can explain all events. Making a decision is an event. Then, Science can explain how I make a decision

Conclusion

C ONGRATULATIONS! You have made it this far because you have applied yourself diligently to practicing for the exam and no doubt improved your potential score considerably! Getting into a good school is a huge step in a journey that might be challenging at times but will be many times more rewarding and fulfilling. That is why being prepared is so important.

Good Luck!

FREE Ebook Version

Download a FREE Ebook version of the publication!

Suitable for tablets, iPad, iPhone, or any smart phone.

Go to http://tinyurl.com/h6thquo

CPSIA information can be obtained
at www.ICGtesting.com
Printed in the USA
LVOW03s0054171017
552623LV00001B/245/P